D0492616

bake-a-boo
BAKERY COOKBOOK

Zoe Berkeley

bake-a-boo
BAKERY COOKBOOK
nostalgic bakes, healthy cakes, party treats

Zoe Berkeley

spruce

An Hachette UK Company

First published in Great Britain in 2010 by
Spruce, a division of Octopus Publishing Group Ltd
Endeavour House, 189 Shaftesbury Avenue, London, WC2H 8JY
www.octopusbooks.co.uk

Copyright © Octopus Publishing Group Ltd 2010
Text copyright © Zoe Athene Berkeley 2010

Zoe Berkeley asserts the moral right to be identified as
the author of this book.

978-1-84601-362-1

All rights reserved. No part of this work may be reproduced or
utilized in any form or by any means, electronic or mechanical,
including photocopying, recording or by any information storage
and retrieval system, without the prior written permission of
the publisher.

A CIP catalogue record of this book is available from the
British Library.

Publisher: Sarah Ford
Managing Editor: Camilla Davis
Designer: Joanna MacGregor
Production: Caroline Alberti
Home Economist: Lorna Brash, Eliza Baird
Photographer: Ian Garlick

Printed and bound in China

10 9 8 7 6 5 4 3 2 1

Publisher's note
Ovens should be preheated to the specific temperature. If using a
fan-assisted oven, follow the manufacturer's instructions for adjusting
the time and temperature.

Both metric and imperial measurements are given for the recipes.
Use one set of measurements only, not a mixture of both.

Contents

♥

Introduction

Bake-a-boo was always a dream for me. When I was 11, my father made me a doll's house, the most perfect I have ever seen. But it wasn't a house, it was a shop with my name over the door. It was filled with food and cakes in cake domes. Then when I was a student I collected vintage china – teacups, teapots and cake stands – simply because I loved them. I'm a huge fan of all things old and sentimental, something that comes from my granny. I used to go round to her house every Sunday for tea. It was always a proper spread, with home-made bread and butter, jam tarts and a layer cake. I recreated those Sunday afternoons when I started bake-a-boo.

I almost fell into baking and wasn't trained at all. I started by making cupcakes for friends. People think baking is hard because it is so precise. Not knowing the rules, I frequently break them, but my motivation has always been about taste and creating something I like to eat. That's why I know if I can do it, then anyone can. I hope this book inspires you to make delicious cakes at home; cakes that taste and look home-made, just the way they should.

Some years ago I was plagued with stomach problems, and was constantly in and out of hospital. I have also suffered from serious eczema since the age of four. I visited a nutritionist who changed my life by telling me to give up gluten and dairy products. During the next six weeks, my body changed, my skin changed and the whole way I felt changed. I was still desperate for cakes and yummy treats, however, so I got creative in my kitchen and eventually ended up with my own bakery. The aim was to make and serve the cakes that people would make at home, real home-made cakes. I always knew how I wanted the shop to look so decorating was easy. I had already built up a huge collection of treasure for it.

Since my diet changed, I knew how hard it was to go out and eat if you have special dietary requirements. I created egg- and sugar-free treats to go with my gluten- and dairy-free creations, in the hope that I would be able to offer something for everyone. I was also keen to serve affordable but wonderful afternoon tea, a special place to go that wasn't a stuffy London hotel. More importantly, I wanted to offer a gluten- and dairy-free afternoon tea. By serving afternoon teas, we naturally fell into hosting and catering for parties of all kinds, both at bake-a-boo and outside venues. I love decorating and making personal touches to make parties extra special.

I really hope I give you some ideas to use at home to make your tea parties even more fabulous. I hope this book continues our mission of offering something for everyone, helping you to make delicious sweet treats at home, free from gluten, dairy, egg and sugar, if necessary, to create intimate and creative tea parties and ways to enjoy treating yourself.

Zoe x

High Tea

Perfect Sandwiches

Dainty little finger sandwiches are the only way to begin your afternoon tea. They are perhaps the most essential part of a proper English afternoon tea and should be just a few mouthfuls of fresh bread with a traditional filling. At bake-a-boo we like to offer both brown and white breads – thick sliced is the easiest to work with and looks the best on the plate.

If your tea party has a theme, you might consider making shaped mini-sandwiches instead of finger sandwiches and fairy bread if there are children. Try hearts, stars, butterflies or seasonal shapes such as chicks at Easter and holly at Christmas. Make the shapes by filling the sandwiches and using biscuit cutters to punch them out.

bake-a-boo's recommended fillings

Cucumber This is the essential finger sandwich, best made with thin-sliced cucumber. Season lightly with salt and cracked black pepper.

Cream cheese Use smooth and creamy full-fat cream cheese. Don't spread it too thick or it will ooze out of the sides of the sandwiches.

Egg mayonnaise We use freshly boiled free-range eggs, peeled, finely chopped and mixed with creamy mayonnaise and a little salt and cracked black pepper. Spread just a thin layer on the bread to avoid oozing.

Smoked salmon Best served with cracked black pepper and a drizzle of lemon juice. You can serve it with cream cheese, too.

Prawn mayonnaise We use fresh peeled prawns mixed with mayonnaise and a squeeze of lemon juice. We also add rocket to our prawn sandwiches.

There are many other great sandwich fillings, including meats and cheeses, roasted vegetables, tuna fish and pâtés. Remember

not to overfill the sandwiches, otherwise the fillings will spill out of the sides when you cut them and make the sandwiches look unattractive.

How to make finger sandwiches

You will need:
- ♥ White and brown thick-sliced fresh bread
- ♥ Butter at room temperature for spreading
- ♥ A sharp knife with a fine serrated edge

Butter a mixture of brown and white bread and make up the sandwiches using the fillings of your choice. Cut the crusts off the sandwiches, then slice each sandwich lengthways into three even fingers; trim off the ends to make them all the same length. You will need a very sharp knife with a fine serrated edge. A serrated bread knife may tear the bread if it is very fresh and soft.

Leon's Scones

These scones are named after our scone master at bake-a-boo, Leon Ockenden. No one makes scones like him. No tea is complete without scones served with lashings of cream and luscious strawberry jam.

375 g (12 oz) self-raising flour, sifted, plus extra for dusting

1½ heaped teaspoons baking powder

75 g (3 oz) butter at room temperature, cubed

2 large free-range eggs, beaten, plus extra for glazing

110 ml (3¾ fl oz) whole milk

Whipped double cream and strawberry jam, to serve

Makes 12–15
Baking time 15 minutes

1 Preheat the oven to 220°C (425°F), Gas Mark 7. Place the flour and baking powder in a large mixing bowl, then rub in the butter with your fingertips until the mixture resembles fine breadcrumbs.

2 Make a well in the centre and pour in the beaten eggs and milk. Mix with a wooden spoon, starting from the centre of the well and stirring outwards until you have a sticky dough. Cover the bowl with clingfilm or a damp cloth and leave to rest for 5 minutes.

3 Lightly dust a work surface with flour, then knead the dough vigorously for 2 minutes until it is smooth and elastic. Rest the dough for another 5 minutes.

4 Roll out the dough to approximately 3.5 cm (1½ inches) thick and use a 6 cm (2½ inch) fluted cutter to cut out the scones, rerolling the trimmings as necessary. Place on a nonstick baking sheet and brush with beaten egg. Bake in the preheated oven for 15 minutes until deliciously golden brown. Serve with whipped cream and strawberry jam.

♥ **Tip:** *To make cheese scones, add 75 g (3 oz) of grated mature Cheddar and a handful of chopped chives to the eggs after you have beaten them, then top the glazed scones with a little more grated cheese before baking.* ♥

Gluten-free Scones

These light and tasty scones are gluten- and dairy-free for allergy sufferers.

450 g (14½ oz) gluten-free flour mix, sifted

3½ teaspoons gluten-free baking powder

1 teaspoon xanthan gum

150 g (5 oz) ground almonds

125 g (4 oz) golden caster sugar

½ teaspoon salt

150 g (5 oz) dairy-free margarine

150 g (5 oz) sultanas

4 large free-range eggs, beaten, plus extra for glazing

Makes 10–12
Baking time 12–15 minutes

1 Preheat the oven to 220°C (425°F), Gas Mark 7, and cover a baking sheet with baking parchment. Place the flour and gluten-free baking powder in a large mixing bowl, then stir in the xanthan gum, ground almonds, sugar and salt. Rub in the margarine with your fingertips until the mixture resembles fine breadcrumbs. Stir in the sultanas.

2 Make a well in the centre and pour in the beaten eggs. Mix with a wooden spoon, starting from the centre of the well and stirring outwards until you have a sticky dough. Wrap the dough in clingfilm and chill in the refrigerator for at least 1 hour.

3 Lightly dust a work surface with flour, roll out the dough to approximately 3.5 cm (1½ inches) thick and use a 6 cm (2½ inch) fluted cutter to cut out the scones, rerolling the trimmings as necessary. Place on the prepared baking sheet and brush with beaten egg. Bake in the preheated oven for 12–15 minutes until deliciously golden brown.

Exotic Fruit Scones

Unlike traditional fruit scones, these are filled with mango, apricots and mixed candied peel for a more exotic flavour.

1 Preheat the oven to 220°C (425°F), Gas Mark 7. Place the flour and baking powder in a large mixing bowl, then rub in the butter with your fingertips until the mixture resembles fine breadcrumbs. Add all the dried fruits and stir to combine.

2 Make a well in the centre and pour in the beaten eggs and milk. Mix with a wooden spoon, starting from the centre of the well and stirring outwards until you have a sticky dough. Cover the bowl with clingfilm or a damp cloth and leave to rest for 5 minutes.

3 Lightly dust a work surface with flour, then knead the dough vigorously for 2 minutes until it is smooth and elastic. Rest the dough for another 5 minutes.

4 Roll out the dough to approximately 3.5 cm (1½ inches) thick and use a 6 cm (2½ inch) fluted cutter to cut out the scones, rerolling the trimmings as necessary. Place on a nonstick baking sheet and brush with beaten egg. Bake in the preheated oven for 15 minutes until deliciously golden brown.

375 g (12 oz) self-raising flour, sifted, plus extra for dusting

1½ heaped teaspoons baking powder

75 g (3 oz) butter at room temperature, cubed

50 g (2 oz) sultanas

25 g (1 oz) dried mango slices, finely chopped

25 g (1 oz) dried apricot slices, finely chopped

15 g (½ oz) mixed candied peel

2 large free-range eggs, beaten, plus extra for glazing

110 ml (3¾ fl oz) whole milk

Makes 12–15
Baking time 15 minutes

Traditional Afternoon Tea

The very English custom of afternoon tea is generally credited to Anna Russell, seventh duchess of Bedford and lifelong friend of Queen Victoria. She believed the gap between lunch and dinner was too long and frequently ordered tea and cakes in her room in the late afternoon. After she invited friends to join her, many ladies picked up on this custom and it became a fashionable way to entertain. Traditional afternoon tea has evolved through the decades, but the elements of sandwiches, cake and pastries remain the same.

Tea etiquette

The key component to any afternoon tea is the tea itself. There are three main types: black, oolong and green teas. The most common examples of black teas are English Breakfast, Darjeeling and Assam, which are usually served with milk or lemon. Oolong teas have a lower caffeine content and are best served with lemon. The most common green teas are gunpowder and jasmine, and are usually served weak without milk.

Loose-leaf tea has the best flavour as it contains larger pieces of leaf; tea bags contain broken leaves to speed up the brewing time. It is worth the extra effort to make a pot of

Boo's High Tea Menu

♥

Finger sandwiches (see page 10)

Leon's Scones with jam and cream
(see page 12)

Boo Fairy Cakes (see pages 19 and 20)

Dainty Lemon Cakes (see page 22)

Chocolate Teapot Biscuits (see page 18)

Additional tempting treats

Traditional Victoria Sponge (see page 24)

Fruit Loaf (see page 25)

Shortbread Triangles (see page 26)

Pear and Custard Slice (see page 27)

loose-leaf tea to complement your delicious home-made cakes. You will need a teapot and strainer for serving. Choose dainty cups and saucers to serve your tea, remembering that tea really does taste better when sipped from bone china.

When washing your teapot, avoid detergents and washing-up liquid, as they can affect the taste of the tea. Simply rinse the pot in water after use and, if it becomes heavily stained, soak in bicarbonate of soda dissolved in hot water.

The perfect cup of tea

First, fill the kettle with fresh cold water and bring to the boil. Swirl the teapot with a little hot water to warm the pot – it really does make the tea taste better. Add one teaspoon of tea per person to the pot, then pour the water over the tea the instant it boils. Allow the tea to brew for about three minutes.

Loose-leaf tea must be poured through a strainer, or you will have leaves floating in your teacup. Tradition has stated that milk should be poured into the cups before the tea to avoid cracking the delicate porcelain. Many people today believe that the milk blends better with the tea that way, but I don't really think it makes much difference to the taste. Serve white and brown sugar lumps (with tongs) and slices of lemon to your guests with their tea.

Chocolate Teapot Biscuits

These cute teapot biscuits are simple but yummy – and their shape makes them perfect for the afternoon tea table.

200 g (7 oz) salted butter at room temperature

175 g (6 oz) golden caster sugar

1 large free-range egg

1 teaspoon vanilla essence

375 g (12 oz) plain flour, sifted

50 g (2 oz) cocoa powder, sifted

Makes 40
Baking time 10 minutes

1 Cream the butter until light and fluffy, then gently beat in the sugar until just combined. Beat in the egg and the vanilla essence, then mix in the flour and cocoa until you have a soft dough. Form into a ball, wrap in clingfilm and chill for at least 2 hours.

2 Preheat the oven to 180°C (350°F), Gas Mark 4, and cover 2 baking sheets with baking parchment. Lightly dust a work surface with flour and roll out the dough to approximately 4 mm (¼ inch) thick. Use a teapot-shaped cutter to cut out the biscuits and carefully lift them onto the prepared baking sheets using a spatula. Bake for 10 minutes until lightly golden at the edges. Leave to cool on the trays.

♥ **Tip:** *If you don't need 40 biscuits, store any unused dough in the freezer for up to 3 months. You can also freeze unbaked biscuits and cook straight from frozen, allowing an extra 2–3 minutes in the oven. Alternatively, freeze the cooked biscuits for up to 1 month.* ♥

Boo Fairy Cakes

The boo fairy cake – perhaps the most understated of all our cupcakes – has always been a bestseller. People always ask how we get our icing so smooth and flat: the secret is revealed here...

1 Preheat the oven to 200°C (400°F), Gas Mark 6, and line a 12-hole muffin tray with paper cases. Lightly cream the butter until light and fluffy, then beat in the caster sugar until just combined. Beat in the eggs one at a time, then the vanilla essence. Gently fold in the flour, taking care not to overwork the mixture.

2 Divide the mixture between the paper cases and cook in the preheated oven for 20 minutes until golden. If the cupcakes have peaked tops, it will be difficult for you to achieve a smooth iced finished, so as soon as you remove them from the oven, gently use the back of a teaspoon to pat the tops down to make them flatter. This will make the cakes denser, but they will still be delicious. Leave to cool in the tray.

3 To make the icing, place the icing sugar in a large mixing bowl, then beat in the water to make a smooth icing. Add a few drops of food colouring, or divide the icing into a number of smaller bowls and colour them all in different shades. Spread the icing over the cooled cakes with the back of a teaspoon, then top with your favourite sprinkles.

125 g (4 oz) butter at room temperature
100 g (3½ oz) golden caster sugar
2 large free-range eggs
1 teaspoon vanilla essence
125 g (4 oz) self-raising flour
Sprinkles, to decorate

Glacé icing
400 g (13 oz) icing sugar, sifted
3 tablespoons water
Food colouring

Makes 12
Baking time 20 minutes

Gluten-free Boo Cakes

This is a gluten- and dairy-free version of our standard vanilla boo fairy cake, so everyone can indulge.

150 g (5 oz) dairy-free margarine

150 g (5 oz) golden caster sugar

2 large free-range eggs

1 teaspoon gluten-free vanilla essence

150 g (5 oz) rice flour, sifted

1 teaspoon gluten-free baking powder

100 g (3½ oz) ready-to-roll fondant icing in a mixture of colours

Dairy-free buttercream

600 g (1 lb 3 oz) icing sugar, sifted, plus extra for dusting

75 g (3 oz) dairy-free margarine

60 ml (2½ fl oz) water

½ teaspoon gluten-free vanilla essence

Pink, blue and yellow food colourings (optional)

Makes 12
Baking time 20 minutes

1 Preheat the oven to 200°C (400°F), Gas Mark 6, and line a 12-hole muffin tray with paper cases. Lightly cream the margarine until smooth and fluffy, then beat in the caster sugar until just combined. Beat in the eggs one at a time, followed by the vanilla essence. Gently fold in the flour and baking powder, taking care not to overwork the mixture.

2 Divide the mixture between the paper cases and cook in the preheated oven for 20 minutes, until the tops are golden. Leave to cool in the tray.

3 To make the buttercream, place the icing sugar in a large mixing bowl and beat in the margarine. Add the water, a little at a time, then stir in the vanilla essence. If you are making different colours, separate the icing into 3 small bowls, add a small drop of food colouring to each and stir well. Be careful when adding colours as they may become too intense.

4 Dust a work surface with icing sugar and roll out the fondant icing. Use icing cutters to cut out flower shapes. Use the back of a teaspoon to swirl buttercream on the tops of the cakes, then top with the fondant icing shapes.

Dainty Lemon Cakes

Mini cupcakes are little mouthfuls of indulgent guilt, ideal for afternoon tea, but also great for children's parties or serving alongside canapés in the evening.

75 g (3 oz) butter at room temperature

75 g (3 oz) golden caster sugar

1 large free-range egg

1 teaspoon vanilla essence

75 g (3 oz) self-raising flour, sifted

Grated rind of ½ lemon

Sugar flowers, to decorate

Lemon icing

450 g (14½ oz) icing sugar, sifted

100 g (3½ oz) butter at room temperature

2 tablespoons lemon juice

1 teaspoon water

Grated rind of ½ lemon

1 drop of natural yellow food colouring

Makes 20
Baking time 10 minutes

1 Preheat the oven to 200°C (400°F), Gas Mark 6, and line a 20-hole mini muffin tray with paper cases. Lightly cream the butter until light and fluffy, then beat in the caster sugar until just combined. Beat in the egg, followed by the vanilla essence. Gently fold in the flour, taking care not to overwork the mixture, then fold in the lemon rind until evenly distributed.

2 Divide the mixture between the paper cases and cook in the preheated oven for 10 minutes until golden. Leave to cool in the tray.

3 To make the icing, place the icing sugar in a large mixing bowl and beat in the butter, followed by the lemon juice a little at a time. Add the measured water to loosen the icing, then mix in the lemon rind and food colouring. Use a teaspoon to swirl the icing over the tops of the cupcakes and top each with a sugar flower.

Traditional Victoria Sponge

This is the mother of all cakes, one everybody loves. Fill with whipped cream and jam if you are eating it on the day you have made it, or use the buttercream below.

250 g (8 oz) butter at room
    temperature
225 g (7½ oz) golden caster sugar
4 large free-range eggs
2 teaspoons vanilla essence
250 g (8 oz) self-raising flour

Buttercream
250 g (8 oz) icing sugar, sifted,
    plus extra for dusting
50 g (2 oz) butter at room
    temperature
½ teaspoon vanilla essence
25 ml (1 fl oz) water

Serves 8–10
Baking time 25 minutes

1 Preheat the oven to 180°C (350°F), Gas Mark 4, and grease and line the bottoms of two 20 cm (8 inch) loose-bottomed cake tins. Lightly cream the butter until light and fluffy, then beat in the caster sugar until just combined. Beat in the eggs one at a time, followed by the vanilla essence. Gently fold in the flour, taking care not to overwork the mixture.

2 Divide the mixture between the tins and bake in the preheated oven for 25 minutes until a skewer inserted into the cakes comes out clean. Leave the cakes to cool before releasing them from the tins.

3 To make the buttercream, place the icing sugar in a large mixing bowl and beat in the butter, vanilla and then the measured water to make a smooth, creamy icing. Once the cakes are cooled, sandwich together with the buttercream. Dust the top of the cake with icing sugar before serving.

Fruit Loaf

This fruit loaf is easy to make and you can use whatever dried fruits you like: simply substitute them weight for weight. Dried apricots and raisins are also good here.

1 Preheat the oven to 180°C (350°F), Gas Mark 4, and grease and lightly flour a loaf tin, approximately 10 cm (4 inches) wide and 20 cm (8 inches) long.

2 Lightly cream the butter until light and fluffy, then beat in the sugar until just combined. Beat in the eggs one at a time, followed by the vanilla essence. Gently fold in the flour, cinnamon and mixed spice, taking care not to overwork the mixture, then fold in the dried fruit and nuts until evenly distributed.

3 Spoon the mixture into the prepared tin, level the surface and cook in the preheated oven for 55 minutes, until a skewer inserted into the cake comes out clean. Leave the cake to cool in the tin, then turn out, slice and serve.

200 g (7 oz) butter at room temperature

200 g (7 oz) light muscovado sugar

3 large free-range eggs

1 teaspoon vanilla essence

200 g (7 oz) self-raising flour, sifted

1 teaspoon ground cinnamon

1 teaspoon ground mixed spice

50 g (2 oz) mixed candied peel

75 g (3 oz) sultanas

75 g (3 oz) dried figs, finely chopped

50 g (2 oz) pecan nuts, roughly chopped

Serves 8–10
Baking time 55 minutes

Shortbread Triangles

Shortbread is a deliciously buttery biscuit, heavenly when dipped in hot tea. This is a real treat that is so easy to make and enjoy.

150 g (5 oz) butter at room
    temperature
125 g (4 oz) golden caster sugar
200 g (7 oz) plain flour, sifted
Pinch of salt
Icing sugar, for dusting

Makes 8
Baking time 45 minutes

1 Preheat the oven to 150°C (300°C), Gas Mark 2, and grease and line the bottom of a 20 cm (8 inch) loose-bottomed cake tin. Lightly cream the butter until light and fluffy, then gently beat in the caster sugar. Add the flour and salt and combine into a stiff mixture.

2 Use your hands to press the mixture evenly into the base of the cake tin, then smooth and level the surface using the back of a metal spoon. Use a knife to score the surface of the shortbread into 8 even triangles, then prick the surface all over with a fork.

3 Bake in the preheated oven for 45 minutes until golden, then leave to cool in the tin. Re-score the cut lines while the shortbread is still warm. Once cooled, remove from the tin and separate the triangles with a knife. Serve dusted with icing sugar.

Pear and Custard Slice

This delicious slice is at its best in autumn when pears are in season. It is great with afternoon tea, but also makes a wonderful dessert with lashings of custard.

1 Preheat the oven to 180°C (350°F), Gas Mark 4, and grease and line the bottom of a shallow baking tin, approximately 33 x 23 cm (13 x 9 inches). Lightly cream the butter until light and fluffy, then beat in the sugar until just combined. Beat in the eggs one at a time, followed by the vanilla essence. Sift together the flour, cinnamon and ground almonds, then gently fold into the mixture, taking care not to overwork.

2 Cut 6 of the pear quarters into cubes and fold into the cake mixture. Spoon the mixture into the tin and spread out evenly. Slice the remaining pears thinly lengthways and arrange in three rows down the length of the tray. Cook in the preheated oven for 45 minutes until golden. Leave to cool in the tin.

3 Once the cake has cooled completely, cut into 12 pieces and arrange on serving plates. Warm the custard until tepid, then drizzle over the cake slices just before serving.

250 g (8 oz) butter at room temperature

225 g (7½ oz) light muscovado sugar

4 large free-range eggs

1 teaspoon vanilla essence

250 g (8 oz) self-raising flour

1 teaspoon ground cinnamon

75 g (3 oz) ground almonds

5 ripe pears, peeled, quartered and cored

150 ml (¼ pint) good-quality fresh custard

Makes 12
Baking time 45 minutes

Tea Parties Galore

Hen party

The ultimate girly gathering…no boys allowed and anything goes. We celebrate hen parties most weekends at bake-a-boo, and they are usually quite civilized affairs: sophisticated with a slightly wild streak.

When planning decorations, think lots of pink and lots of glitter and hearts. Baby pink just won't do! Use pink and red plates, teacups and napkins, and serve your chosen tipple (even if it is only water) in martini glasses. Sprinkle the table with hearts and lips confetti, making sure you have a pale-coloured tablecloth to show the impact of the confetti.

A hot pink feather boa for each hen and individual favours are essential. For these, fill small boxes with glamorous gifts such as chocolate hearts, mini pampering products, red nail varnish and lipstick. Wrap each individual box in hot pink tissue paper and embellish with bows, feather tassels, ribbons, sequins and beads.

Hen Party Menu

♥

Lip-shaped mini sandwiches (see page 10)

Mini scones with jam and cream
(see page 12)

Party Popcorn Buckets (see page 32)

Cosmopolitan Cupcakes (see page 33)

Glamorous Glitter Brownies (see page 34)

Sparkly Chocolate Truffles (see page 36)

Strawberry Vodka Jellies (see page 37)

A hen tea party is the perfect place for girly chats and giggles, but activities and games always add to the fun. Decorate a pretty book with photographs and personal things before the party, then ask each hen to fill a page with tips on marriage and a personal message for the bride-to-be. Or, if you feel like getting crafty, make a wedding veil for the bride out of netting, lace, beads and flowers – have fun together designing it.

Wedding tea

Weddings can be stressful occasions and a delightful, intimate tea that oozes charm and romance is a wonderful antidote.

For truly romantic lighting, set tables amongst twinkling fairy lights, then adorn the tables with vintage-print cloths scattered with doilies and strewn with rose petals. Proper teacups and saucers are essential: you can collect mismatched second-hand china, plates and cake stands to add real charm to your tables. Serve sugar lumps in pretty bowls with tongs, and milk and water infused with lemon in pretty glass or china jugs.

Complete the look with romantic touches, such as flower posies in vintage teapots, tea glasses or even pretty milk jugs. Tie different coloured ribbons around the flower posies and then give your guests a piece of ribbon to tie around their wrists so they can identify their table.

If you are offering personalized favours to guests, stick with the romantic theme. Consider hand-tied bags or netting filled with rose pot pourri, or individually-decorated envelopes filled with seeds of the chosen flowers for your wedding, which guests can plant at home. Alternatively, collect individual trinket items cheaply from markets, charity shops and car boot sales. Keep an eye out for items to make really individual gifts for your guests to treasure.

Wedding Tea Menu

♥

Heart-shaped sandwiches (see page 10)

Exotic Fruit Scones with jam and cream (see page 15)

Strawberry Shortcakes (see page 43)

Florentines (see page 38)

Rose-scented Cupcakes (see page 42)

Cherub Biscuits (see page 40)

Feather-light Cream Cake (see page 41)

Party Popcorn Buckets

Everybody loves popcorn. Either sprinkle with salt or sugar, or use one of the coatings below. One is only sweetened with agave nectar, a great sugar substitute available in health food shops, larger supermarkets or online.

100 g (3½ oz) popping corn
2 tablespoons sunflower oil
Sugar or salt, for coating (optional)

Chocolate coating

4 teaspoons cocoa powder
4 tablespoons caster sugar
2 tablespoons agave nectar

Agave cinnamon coating

1 teaspoon ground cinnamon
6 tablespoons agave nectar

Serves 4–6

1 Cover the bottom of a large saucepan with the oil and place over a high heat. Pour in the popping corn and stir well to coat in the oil. Cover with a heavy lid or you will end up with a popcorn explosion. It will take about a minute for the popping to start.

2 Shake the pan a few times while it is popping, and take off the heat as soon as the popping stops. Add a little sugar or salt, or make one of the coatings below. Serve the popcorn in cardboard popcorn buckets, available from most party shops.

To make the chocolate coating, mix together the cocoa and sugar and add to the pan of popcorn as soon as it comes off the heat. Stir thoroughly until the sugar starts to dissolve. Pour in the agave nectar and mix to coat. Leave to cool a little before serving.

To make the agave cinnamon coating, sprinkle over the cinnamon as soon as the popcorn comes off the heat and mix thoroughly. Pour in the agave nectar and mix to coat.

Cosmopolitan Cupcakes

This is one of the girliest cupcakes ever! Perfect for a hen party, served with Cosmopolitan cocktails.

1 Preheat the oven to 200°C (400°F), Gas Mark 6, and line a 12-hole muffin tray with paper cases. Lightly cream the butter until light and fluffy, then beat in the caster sugar until just combined. Beat in the eggs one at a time. Gently fold in the flour, taking care not to overwork the mixture, then fold in the jam until well mixed.

2 Divide the mixture between the paper cases and cook in the preheated oven for 20 minutes until golden. Leave to cool in the tray.

3 To make the icing, place the icing sugar in a large mixing bowl, then beat in the butter and then the Triple Sec and food colouring to make a smooth, creamy icing. Use the back of a teaspoon to spread the icing over the cakes and top each with a cocktail umbrella.

125 g (4 oz) butter at room temperature

100 g (3½ oz) golden caster sugar

2 large free-range eggs

125 g (4 oz) self-raising flour, sifted

2 tablespoons cranberry jam

12 cocktail umbrellas, to decorate

Cosmopolitan icing

500 g (1 lb) icing sugar, sifted

100 g (3½ oz) butter at room temperature

75 ml (3 fl oz) Triple Sec or other orange liqueur

1 teaspoon pink food colouring

Makes 12
Baking time 20 minutes

Glamorous Glitter Brownies

To achieve the biggest impact with the glitter topping, these brownies do not have a crispy top. However, the surprise pieces of pink wafer deliver a satisfying crunch.

200 g (7 oz) butter, melted

65 g (2½ oz) cocoa powder

3 large free-range eggs

200 g (7 oz) golden caster sugar

1 teaspoon vanilla essence

75 g (3 oz) self-raising flour, sifted

6 pink wafer biscuits, roughly broken

Edible pink and gold glitter, to decorate

Makes 12
Baking time 35 minutes

1   Preheat the oven to 180°C (350°F), Gas Mark 4, and grease and line the bottom of a shallow baking tin, approximately 20 cm (8 inches) square. Mix the melted butter with the cocoa, then set aside to cool for at least 10 minutes.

2   Lightly whisk the eggs with the sugar and vanilla essence, then beat in the cooled cocoa mixture. Gently fold in the flour, then the pieces of pink wafer. Pour the mixture into the prepared tin and bake in the centre of the preheated oven for 35 minutes. It should still be a bit sticky.

3   Leave to cool in the tin, then remove and cut into 12 pieces. Sprinkle with gold and pink glitter before serving.

Sparkly Chocolate Truffles

These melt-in-the-mouth truffles make a great party treat for adults and children alike, and the kids will love to help you make them.

100 g (3½ oz) milk chocolate,
   broken into pieces
150 g (5 oz) ground almonds
1 tablespoon double cream
Edible pink glitter, for dusting
12 heart sprinkles, to decorate

Makes 12

1 Cover a baking sheet with baking parchment. Melt the chocolate in a heatproof bowl over a saucepan of gently simmering water, stirring regularly.

2 Once the chocolate has completely melted, remove from the heat and stir in the almonds. The mixture will become quite stiff, so add the cream to loosen it a little. Use your hands to roll the mixture into 12 smooth balls and place on the prepared baking sheet.

3 Dust a plate with the glitter and roll the truffles in it until evenly coated. Push a single heart sprinkle into the top of each truffle and chill in the refrigerator for 1 hour.

Strawberry Vodka Jellies

Strawberry jelly is a nostalgic nursery favourite, but this version is for grown-ups only.

1 Pour the boiling water into a large measuring jug, add the jelly and stir until it has completely dissolved. Leave to cool for 10 minutes.

2 Mix the measured cold water and vodka, then add to the jelly and stir well. Divide the jelly between 6 glasses or small dishes and drop in some raspberries and sliced strawberries. Chill in the refrigerator for at least 6 hours, or preferably overnight. The length of time it takes for the jellies to set will depend on their size.

300 ml (½ pint) boiling water

Strawberry jelly powder or cubes, enough to make 600 ml (1 pint) jelly

150 ml (¼ pint) cold water

150 ml (¼ pint) good-quality vodka

Raspberries and sliced strawberries, to decorate

Serves 6

Florentines

Florentines are in a league of their own. These are dairy- and gluten-free, but you can replace the margarine with butter and the gluten-free flour with normal plain flour.

50 g (2 oz) dairy-free margarine

50 g (2 oz) light muscovado sugar

2 teaspoons runny honey

50 g (2 oz) flaked almonds, roughly chopped

25 g (1 oz) shelled, unsalted pistachios, roughly chopped

25 g (1 oz) gluten-free glacé cherries, roughly chopped

25 g (1 oz) mixed candied peel, roughly chopped

25 g (1 oz) sultanas, roughly chopped

50 g (2 oz) gluten-free flour mix, sifted

100 g (3½ oz) dairy-free chocolate (plain, white or milk)

Makes 10
Baking time 15 minutes

1 Preheat the oven to 180°C (350°F), Gas Mark 4, and cover a baking sheet with baking parchment.

2 Melt the margarine in a small saucepan over a low heat, then add the sugar and honey and stir over the heat until melted. Transfer to a mixing bowl to cool.

3 Stir the nuts and dried fruits into the margarine mixture, then fold in the flour until well combined. Use your hands to roll the mixture into 10 balls, then space them out on the baking sheet, flattening them slightly with your fingers as you go. Bake in the preheated oven for 15 minutes until lightly golden, then leave to cool on the baking sheet.

4 Melt the chocolate in a bowl over a pan of lightly simmering water, then use a spoon to spread it on the underneath of each florentine. Leave to set with the chocolate facing up.

Cherub Biscuits

Cherubs symbolize love, so these delightful little biscuits are perfect for a romantic tea party, a gift for your loved one or as favours for a wedding party.

200 g (7 oz) salted butter at room temperature

175 g (6 oz) golden caster sugar

1 large free-range egg

1 teaspoon almond essence

425 g (14 oz) plain flour, sifted, plus extra for dusting

Makes 40
Baking time 10 minutes

1 Cream the butter until light and fluffy, then gently beat in the sugar until just combined. Beat in the egg and the almond essence, then mix in the flour until you have a soft dough. Form into a ball, wrap in clingfilm and chill for at least 2 hours.

2 Preheat the oven to 180°C (350°F), Gas Mark 4, and cover 2 baking sheets with baking parchment. Lightly dust a work surface with flour and roll out the dough to approximately 4 mm (¼ inch) thick. Use a cherub-shaped cutter to cut out the biscuits and carefully lift them onto the prepared baking sheets using a spatula.

3 Bake for 10 minutes until lightly golden at the edges, then leave to cool on the trays. See the tip on page 18 for storing any leftover dough or biscuits.

Feather-light Cream Cake

This light and fluffy sponge is made with fresh cream, then sandwiched with more whipped cream to create a fresh-tasting treat.

1   Preheat the oven to 180°C (350°F), Gas Mark 4, and grease and line the bottoms of two 20 cm (8 inch) loose-bottomed cake tins. You will need 3 mixing bowls. Sift the flour, salt and baking powder into one mixing bowl and set aside. Pour 250 ml (8 fl oz) of the cream into the second bowl and stir in the vanilla essence. In the final bowl, beat the eggs until they start to thicken, then slowly whisk in the caster sugar.

2   Fold one-third of the dry mixture into the egg mixture, then beat in one-third of the cream mixture. Continue until you have combined all the ingredients and you have a light and creamy batter.

3   Divide the mixture between both of the cake tins and bake immediately before any of the air escapes from the mixture. Cook in the preheated oven for 25–30 minutes until a skewer inserted into the cakes comes out clean. Leave the cakes to cool before releasing them from the tins.

4   Once the cakes are fully cooled, whip the remaining cream and use to sandwich the cakes together. Dust the top of the cake with icing sugar and serve.

200 g (7 oz) self-raising flour
½ teaspoon salt
2 teaspoons baking powder
350 ml (12 fl oz) double cream
1 teaspoon vanilla essence
2 large free-range eggs
200 g (7 oz) caster sugar
Icing sugar, for dusting

Serves 8–10
Baking time 25–30 minutes

Rose-scented Cupcakes

These cupcakes are imbued with rose, the scent of romance. They are perfect for a wedding tea or any other romantic occasion.

125 g (4 oz) butter at room
 temperature

100 g (3½ oz) golden caster sugar

2 large free-range eggs

150 g (5 oz) self-raising flour,
 sifted

50 ml (2 fl oz) rose syrup

12 red or pink sugar roses, to
 decorate

Rosewater icing

500 g (1 lb) icing sugar, sifted

100 g (3½ oz) butter at room
 temperature

50 ml (2 fl oz) rosewater

Drop of pink food colouring

Makes 12
Baking time 20 minutes

1 Preheat the oven to 200°C (400°F), Gas Mark 6, and line a 12-hole muffin tray with paper cases. Lightly cream the butter until light and fluffy, then beat in the caster sugar until just combined. Beat in the eggs one at a time. Gently fold in the flour, taking care not to overwork the mixture, then fold in the rose syrup until well combined.

2 Divide the mixture between the paper cases and cook in the preheated oven for 20 minutes or until the cakes are golden. Leave to cool in the tray.

3 To make the icing, place the icing sugar in a bowl and beat in the butter, then the rosewater and pink food colouring to make a smooth, creamy icing. Use the back of a teaspoon to spread the cooled cakes with the butter icing, then top each cake with a sugar rose.

Strawberry Shortcakes

This quintessentially English summertime treat is halfway between a scone and a biscuit, sandwiched together with fresh cream and strawberries.

1   Preheat the oven to 200°C (400°F), Gas Mark 6. Place the flour in a large mixing bowl, then rub in the butter with your fingertips until the mixture resembles fine breadcrumbs. Stir in the caster sugar, then the beaten egg. Use your hands to bring the mixture together into a soft dough and knead lightly for 1 minute.

2   Lightly dust a work surface with flour and roll out the dough to about 1.5 cm (¾ inch) thick. Cut out 6 rounds with a 6 cm (2½ inch) fluted cutter and place on a nonstick baking sheet. Brush the tops of the shortcakes with beaten egg and cook in the preheated oven for 15 minutes. Leave to cool on the tray.

3   Slice the shortcakes in half, spread the bottom halves with cream and top with sliced strawberries. Arrange the tops of the shortcakes on the strawberries at a slight angle, dust with icing sugar and serve.

250 g (8 oz) self-raising flour, sifted, plus extra for dusting

100 g (3½ oz) butter at room temperature, cubed

50 g (2 oz) golden caster sugar

1 large free-range egg, beaten, plus extra for glazing

100 ml (3½ fl oz) double cream, whipped

18 strawberries, sliced

Icing sugar, for dusting

Makes 6
Baking time 15 minutes

Baby shower

This is a time for friends and loved ones to really pamper a mum-to-be; a time to share a very special moment and to make her feel really excited about this new phase of her life.

A delightful afternoon tea party is the perfect way to celebrate this occasion, and it should be a very feminine affair filled with cutesy touches. If you know the sex of the baby you can incorporate this in your colours and decorations, but a combination of baby pink and powder blue is a great scheme for any baby shower.

Decorate the table with pink and blue plates, teacups and saucers. Fresh flowers in shades of pink, blue and touches of yellow are essential: try using pink roses, forget-me-nots, bluebells and yellow freesias. Scatter tables with plastic miniature safety pins and dummies, and pastel confetti.

Offer favours to all your guests in the form of pastel-coloured chocolate eggs wrapped in cellophane bags with pink and blue ribbons and buttons. It's a good idea to mark the bags with name tags, as guests at a baby shower are often from different circles of friends and may not know each other. A delightful final touch is a make-a-wish jar or box. This is a great keepsake for the mum-to-be to take away with her as a memory of the day. Decorate a jar with a tag stating 'make-a-wish' and fill it with pastel-coloured blank cards. Each guest should write a wish for the baby and place it in the jar.

Baby Shower Menu

♥

Finger sandwiches (see page 10)

Mini scones with jam and cream (see page 12)

White Chocolate-dipped Strawberries
(see page 50)

Heavenly Macaroons (see page 46)

Butterscotch Baby Shower Cakes (see page 48)

Christening tea

A christening is a lovely celebration. Often even those who are not religious want to have some kind of occasion like a baby blessing or naming ceremony as a chance to meet with friends and celebrate their new life with their baby. A tea party with close friends, with simple-to-make cakes and a cup of delicious tea is easy to prepare and enjoyable.

Neutral cream colours are perfect for a christening tea table. I usually take inspiration from a traditional christening gown: think antique cream, satin and lace. China with simple gold patterns or trims looks perfect, complemented with church candles in all different sizes surrounded by cream roses and lilies. Scatter cream rose petals and loose faux pearls on the table.

Create personal but simple favours for your guests. Buy loose tea in bulk and create small bags of tea with personalized labels featuring the child's name and date of the event.

A lovely thing to do as part of a christening or baby blessing is to plant a tree. It will grow with your baby and be a lovely thing for your child to see when he or she is older. Involve your guests by giving them each a small pouch of fine glitter and ask everyone to scatter it on the earth so each person adds some magic to the tree.

Christening Tea Menu

♥

Finger sandwiches (see page 10)

Mini cheese scones (see page 12)

Fluffy Pink Meringues (see page 49)

Blondies (see page 50)

Autumnal Apple Cake (see page 51)

Heavenly Macaroons

These mini macaroons are chewy bites of sweet heaven; they are also free from gluten and dairy. These are my sister's all-time favourite teatime treat.

1 large free-range egg white
85 g (3¼ oz) golden caster sugar
100 g (3½ oz) ground almonds
Orange flower water, for rolling
12 whole blanched almonds

Makes 12
Baking time 10 minutes

1 Preheat the oven to 180°C (350°F), Gas Mark 4, and cover a baking sheet with baking parchment. Mix the egg white with the sugar until well combined, then fold in the ground almonds to make a gooey, sticky mixture.

2 Wet the palms of your hands with orange flower water to allow you to handle the sticky mixture more easily. Roll the mixture into 12 equal balls and place a good distance apart on the prepared baking sheet. Flatten lightly with your fingers, then place a single blanched almond in the centre of each.

3 Cook in the preheated oven for 10 minutes then leave to cool on the baking sheet. Remove with a palette knife and serve.

Butterscotch Baby Shower Cakes

Richly flavoured, these butterscotch cupcakes are a real treat. The pretty ribbon decoration makes them perfect for a baby shower tea party.

125 g (4 oz) butter at room temperature

100 g (3½ oz) golden caster sugar

2 large free-range eggs

4 tablespoons butterscotch ice-cream sauce

125 g (4 oz) self-raising flour, sifted

Butterscotch icing

500 g (1 lb) icing sugar, sifted

100 g (3½ oz) butterscotch mousse powder

100 g (3½ oz) butter at room temperature

50 ml (2 fl oz) water

To decorate

Pink and blue satin or gingham ribbons

12 fudge cubes

Makes 12
Baking time 20 minutes

1 Preheat the oven to 200°C (400°F), Gas Mark 6, and line a 12-hole muffin tray with paper cases. Lightly cream the butter until light and fluffy, then beat in the caster sugar until just combined. Beat in the eggs one at a time, then the butterscotch sauce. Gently fold in the flour, taking care not to overwork the mixture.

2 Divide the mixture between the paper cases and cook in the preheated oven for 20 minutes or until the cakes are golden. Leave to cool in the tray.

3 To make the icing, place the icing sugar in a bowl and mix in the mousse powder. Beat in the butter, then the measured water to make a smooth, creamy icing. Use the back of a teaspoon to spread the icing over the tops of the cakes.

4 Tie a short length of pink ribbon round one end of a cocktail stick and finish in a neat bow. Repeat with some blue ribbon. Skewer a cube of fudge on the other end of the stick and push the stick down through the fudge and into the top of one of the cakes. Repeat with the other cakes.

Fluffy Pink Meringues

This recipe was given to me by my mother, the queen of meringues. It makes 15 mini teatime meringues, but the same mixture can be used to make one large pavlova, just increase the cooking time to 2 hours.

1 Preheat the oven to 150°C (300°F), Gas Mark 2, and cover 2 baking sheets with baking parchment. Use a lead-free pencil to draw 5 cm (2 inch) circles on the baking parchment, spacing them at least 10 cm (4 inches) apart to allow space for the meringues to spread.

2 Place the egg whites in a large mixing bowl, set a hand-held electric whisk to a slow speed and whisk the eggs for about a minute and a half. This slow start incorporates more air into the mixture. Increase the speed to fast and whisk until soft peaks form. Do not overwhisk or the whites will collapse.

3 While continuing to whisk on a medium speed, add the sugar, a tablespoon at a time, followed by the vanilla essence and food colouring. Continue until the mixture is stiff and you can turn the bowl upside down without it falling out.

4 Spoon the meringue into the circles, leaving the tops peaked. Cook in the preheated oven for 20 minutes, then turn off the oven and leave the meringues inside without opening the door for at least 6 hours or until completely cold.

3 large free-range egg whites
175 g (6 oz) caster sugar
1 drop of vanilla essence
1 teaspoon red food colouring

Makes 15
Baking time 20 minutes

Blondies

400 g (13 oz) white chocolate

100 g (3½ oz) butter

100 g (3½ oz) golden caster sugar

1 teaspoon vanilla essence

3 large free-range eggs

225 g (7½ oz) self-raising flour, sifted

Makes 12
Baking time 35 minutes

1 Preheat the oven to 160°C (325°F), Gas Mark 3, and grease and line the bottom of a shallow baking tin, approximately 20 cm (8 inches) square. Melt 300 g (10 oz) of the white chocolate and the butter in a heatproof bowl over a saucepan of gently simmering water, stirring regularly. Remove from the heat.

2 Beat in the sugar and vanilla essence, then the eggs one at a time. Fold in the flour until well combined. Chop the remaining chocolate into chunks and stir into the mixture, then transfer it to the prepared tin and level with a spoon.

3 Cook in the preheated oven for 35 minutes, until the top appears crispy and a skewer inserted into the cake comes out clean. Leave to cool in the tin, then remove and cut into 12 pieces.

Chocolate-dipped Strawberries

20 large strawberries

125 g (4 oz) milk, white or plain dark chocolate

Sugar strand sprinkles, for dipping (optional)

Makes 20

1 Melt the chocolate in a heatproof bowl over a saucepan of gently simmering water, stirring regularly. Cover a large plate with baking parchment and shake some sugar sprinkles on another plate, if using.

2 Hold the strawberries by their leaves and dip them, one by one, into the melted chocolate until they are half covered.

3 If using sugar sprinkles, dip the chocolatey sides of the strawberries into the sprinkles to cover. Place the chocolate-covered strawberries on the baking parchment-covered plate and chill in the refrigerator for 1 hour to harden.

Autumnal Apple Cake

This is a deliciously moist cake, perfectly complemented by a pot of tea by a cosy fire on an autumn afternoon.

1 Preheat the oven to 180°C (350°F), Gas Mark 4, and grease and line the bottom of a 20 cm (8 inch) loose-bottomed cake tin. Cream the butter and muscovado sugar together until smooth and creamy, then beat in the eggs one at a time.

2 Stir in the apples and sultanas, then gently fold in the flour and cinnamon until well combined. Transfer the mixture to the prepared cake tin and level with a spoon.

3 Arrange the apple slices for the topping in a neat fan all the way around the outer edge of the cake, then make a circle in the centre. Sprinkle the apples with the demerara sugar, then cook in the preheated oven for 45 minutes until a skewer inserted into the cake comes out clean. Leave to cool in the tin, then release and serve dusted with icing sugar.

175 g (6 oz) butter at room temperature

150 g (5 oz) light muscovado sugar

3 large free-range eggs

200 g (7 oz) apples, peeled, cored and sliced

100 g (3½ oz) sultanas

175 g (6 oz) self-raising flour, sifted

1 teaspoon ground cinnamon

Icing sugar, for dusting

Topping

2 apples, peeled, cored and finely sliced

2 teaspoons demerara sugar

Serves 8–10
Baking time 45 minutes

A Day to Remember

Valentine's Day

Seen by some as corny, but really Valentine's Day is a lovely celebration. You don't have to be extravagant to show your loved-one how you feel; simple personal touches are worth so much more. They say that the way to a man's heart is through his stomach so try making edible gifts. Try little cellophane bags tied with ribbon and filled with Rose Petal Biscuits, or make Brownie Love Hearts and present one in a pretty box or just on a plate for breakfast. If you have a little more time, you could even organize a tea party for your beloved with a selection of cakes served on a table scattered with red rose petals, heart confetti and, of course, candles to set the mood.

Valentine's Suggestions

♥

Heart-shaped mini sandwiches (see page 10)

Chocolate Raspberry Heart (see page 56)

Brownie Love Hearts (see page 58)

Rose Petal Biscuits (see page 59)

Passion Fruit Cake (see page 60)

Raspberry Cupcakes (see page 62)

Banana and Sultana Hearts (see page 63)

Mother's Day

Mother's Day is the busiest day of the year for us at bake-a-boo, which just goes to show that preparing a lovely afternoon tea is the perfect way to show your mother how special she is. Classic cakes like coffee cake and lemon drizzle cakes are perfect, especially as many people celebrate this occasion along with grandma too.

Don't forget to dress up for your Mother's Day tea, in pearls and lace gloves, and have a real giggle among the generations. Make a special table with vintage china and a pretty pot of refreshing loose tea – you will have to get your tea cosy out for this one!

Mother's Day Tea Menu

♥

Finger sandwiches (see page 10)

Exotic Fruit Scones served with jam and cream (see page 15)

Lemon Drizzle Cake (see page 64)

Classic Coffee Cake (see page 66)

Earl Grey Cupcakes (see page 71)

Apple and Date Cake (see page 67)

Easter

Easter is probably my favourite occasion. My sister and I call it 'the most wonderful time of the year' – I know those are the words from a Christmas song, but for me Easter is just that. I love the colours, the flowers and the feeling at this time of year when everything seems more positive and fresh. It is also a great excuse to make and enjoy delicious cakes. Obviously chocolate is usually the order of the day, but for something different try a traditional Simnel Cake – a wonderful light, fruity cake, topped with marzipan. Or make bunny-shaped biscuits for the children or as gifts for friends. Easter is a time to fill the house with blooming flowers, decorate your own eggs and, of course, make delicious Easter treats.

Easter Suggestions

♥

Chick- and bunny-shaped sandwiches
(see page 10)

Simnel Cake (see page 72)

Chocolate Mint Cupcakes (see page 73)

Easter Bunny Biscuits (see page 74)

Vegan Chocolate and Nut Cake (see page 69)

Chocolate Chip Tray Bake (see page 70)

Father's Day

Father's Day is a time to make your dad feel special. It is often hard to buy gifts for fathers, especially if they are anything like mine who always says he has everything he needs! Making a cake is a great solution to this problem, and a nice way to give a personal gift to your father, which he will really enjoy. You can spoil him by having a small family tea party, or you could make him an edible gift such as delicious Cappuccino Cakes presented in a pretty box with a handmade card. This is really easy to do and you don't need to spend much, but there is a lot of thought involved. You could even pipe a message on the cupcakes, or just his name, if you like.

Father's Day Tea Menu

♥

Finger sandwiches (see page 10)

Leon's Scones with jam and cream
(see page 12)

Kimberley's Cappuccino Cakes (see page 76)

Vegan Banana Cake (see page 77)

Light Hazelnut Cake (see page 68)

Chocolate Raspberry Heart

This is the perfect Valentine treat for your loved one. The feather-light chocolate sponge is complemented by raspberries, ideal for serving at the end of a romantic meal.

250 g (8 oz) butter at room temperature

250 g (8 oz) caster sugar

4 large free-range eggs

1 teaspoon vanilla essence

225 g (7½ oz) self-raising flour, sifted

75 g (3 oz) cocoa powder

175 g (6 oz) raspberries

50 g (2 oz) milk chocolate chips

Edible coloured glitter, to decorate

Chocolate buttercream

500 g (1 lb) icing sugar, sifted

25 g (1 oz) cocoa powder

100 g (3½ oz) butter at room temperature

60 ml (2½ fl oz) water

Serves 8–10
Baking time 25 minutes

1 Preheat the oven to 180°C (350°F), Gas Mark 4, and grease and line the bottoms of 2 heart-shaped cake tins, approximately 20 cm (8 inches) across and 5 cm (2 inches) deep.

2 Cut 75 g (3 oz) of the raspberries in half. Lightly cream the butter until light and fluffy, then beat in the caster sugar until just combined. Beat in the eggs one at a time, followed by the vanilla essence. Add the sifted flour and cocoa and fold in gently until well combined. Finally, fold in the chocolate chips and halved raspberries.

3 Divide the mixture between the tins and bake in the preheated oven for 25 minutes until a skewer inserted into the cake comes out clean. Leave the cakes to cool before releasing them from the tins.

4 To make the buttercream, place the icing sugar and cocoa in a large mixing bowl and beat in the butter. Add the water, a little at a time, to form a smooth icing. Sandwich the hearts together using half the buttercream, then leave to set for at least 30 minutes.

5 Smooth the remaining buttercream over the top of the cake, then cover with the remaining raspberries and sprinkle with glitter.

Brownie Love Hearts

Pipe your beloved's name on these rich chocolate brownie hearts, wrap them in cellophane and ribbon, and present them as a delicious token of your love.

400 g (13 oz) butter, melted

150 g (5 oz) cocoa powder

6 large free-range eggs

375 g (12 oz) golden caster sugar

2 teaspoons vanilla essence

150 g (5 oz) self-raising flour, sifted

Red or white writing icing tube

Makes 10–12
Baking time 45–50 minutes

1 Preheat the oven to 180°C (350°F), Gas Mark 4, and grease and line the bottom of a shallow baking tin, approximately 33 x 23 cm (13 x 9 inches). Mix the melted butter with the cocoa, then set aside to cool for at least 10 minutes.

2 Lightly whisk the eggs with the sugar and vanilla essence, then beat in the cooled cocoa mixture. Gently fold in the flour. Pour the mixture into the prepared tin and bake in the centre of the preheated oven for 45–50 minutes. It should still be a bit sticky. Leave to cool in the tin.

3 Once removed from the tin, use a 6 cm (2½ inch) heart-shaped biscuit cutter to cut out 10–12 hearts. There will be quite a lot of waste, but you can treat this as Cook's perks. Use the writing icing tube to pipe your beloved's name on the brownies and leave the icing to harden for 2–3 hours before gift wrapping.

Rose Petal Biscuits

These heart-shaped, rose-scented biscuits have pretty pink flecks of rose petal, the perfect Valentine gift.

1 Cream the butter until light and fluffy, then gently beat in the sugar until just combined. Beat in the egg and the rose syrup, then mix in the rose petals and flour until you have a soft dough. Make sure the rose petals are evenly distributed, then form the dough into a ball, wrap in clingfilm and chill for at least 2 hours.

2 Preheat the oven to 180°C (350°F), Gas Mark 4, and cover 2 baking sheets with baking parchment. Lightly dust a work surface with flour and roll out the dough to approximately 4 mm (¼ inch) thick.

3 Use a 6 cm (2½ inch) heart-shaped cutter to cut out the biscuits and carefully lift them onto the prepared baking sheets using a spatula. Bake for 10 minutes until lightly golden at the edges. Leave to cool on the trays. See the tip on page 18 for storing any leftover dough or biscuits.

200 g (7 oz) salted butter at room temperature

175 g (6 oz) golden caster sugar

1 large free-range egg

1 teaspoon rose syrup

2 tablespoons crystallized rose petals, crushed

425 g (14 oz) plain flour, sifted, plus extra for dusting

Makes 40
Baking time 10 minutes

Passion Fruit Cake

Suitable for allergy and intolerance sufferers as well as coeliacs, this cake oozes passion; a special way to show your love for someone on Valentine's Day.

300 g (10 oz) dairy-free margarine

250 g (8 oz) golden caster sugar

4 large free-range eggs

1 teaspoon gluten-free vanilla essence

300 g (10 oz) rice flour, sifted

2 teaspoons gluten-free baking powder

1 passion fruit

Grated rind of ½ orange

100 g (4 oz) each of red and baby pink ready-to-roll fondant icing

Passion fruit buttercream

625 g (1¼ lb) icing sugar, sifted, plus extra for dusting

75 g (3 oz) dairy-free margarine

1 passion fruit

50 ml (2 fl oz) water

Serves 8–10
Baking time 25 minutes

1 Preheat the oven to 180°C (350°F), Gas Mark 4, and grease and line the bottoms of two 20 cm (8 inch) loose-bottomed cake tins. Cream the margarine until light and fluffy, then beat in the caster sugar until just combined. Beat in the eggs one at a time, followed by the vanilla essence.

2 Gently fold in the flour and baking powder, taking care not to overwork the batter. Fold in the passion fruit seeds and flesh and the orange rind, then divide the mixture between the prepared tins, level the surface and cook in the preheated oven for 25 minutes until a skewer inserted into the cakes comes out clean. Leave the cakes to cool before releasing them from the tins.

3 To make the buttercream, place the icing sugar in a large mixing bowl and beat in the margarine and the passion fruit seeds and flesh. Slowly add the measured water to make a smooth, creamy icing. Use half the buttercream to sandwich the cakes together, then leave to set for 30 minutes. Use a flat spatula to spread the remaining icing on top of the cake.

4 Dust a work surface with icing sugar and roll out the red fondant icing. Use a small heart-shaped cutter to cut out some red hearts, then repeat with the pink icing. Arrange the red and pink hearts alternately on top of the cake.

Raspberry Cupcakes

These gluten- and dairy-free cupcakes are a bestseller at bake-a-boo. The raspberries make the cakes deliciously moist, and the naturally pink icing is sweet and fruity.

150 g (5 oz) dairy-free margarine

150 g (5 oz) golden caster sugar

2 large free-range eggs

1 teaspoon vanilla essence

150 g (5 oz) rice flour

1 teaspoon gluten-free baking powder

200 g (7 oz) canned raspberries in fruit juice, drained and juice reserved

12 fresh raspberries, to decorate

Raspberry buttercream

500 g (1 lb) icing sugar, sifted

50 g (2 oz) dairy-free margarine

50 ml (2 fl oz) raspberry juice from the can

Makes 12

Baking time 20 minutes

1 Preheat the oven to 200°C (400°F), Gas Mark 6, and line a 12-hole muffin tray with paper cases. Lightly cream the margarine until smooth and fluffy, then beat in the caster sugar until just combined. Beat in the eggs one at a time, followed by the vanilla essence. Gently fold in the flour and baking powder, taking care not to overwork the mixture. Stir in the drained canned raspberries.

2 Divide the mixture between the paper cases and cook in the preheated oven for 20 minutes, until the tops are golden. Leave to cool in the tray.

3 To make the buttercream, place the icing sugar in a large mixing bowl and beat in the margarine. Slowly stir in the raspberry juice until well combined. Use the back of a teaspoon to spread the icing on top of the cupcakes. Top each cake with a fresh raspberry.

Banana and Sultana Hearts

As well as being free from gluten and dairy, these cakes contain no sugar. They are sweetened with agave nectar, suitable for those with type 2 diabetes.

1 Preheat the oven to 180°C (350°F), Gas Mark 4, and grease and line the bottom of a 23 cm (9 inch) loose-bottomed cake tin. Cream the mashed bananas with the margarine and agave nectar until well combined. Beat in the eggs one at a time, then fold in the sultanas and ground almonds.

2 Gently fold in the flour, baking powder and cinnamon until well combined, taking care not to overwork the mixture. Transfer to the prepared tin, level the surface and cook in the preheated oven for 45 minutes until the top begins to brown and a skewer inserted into the cake comes out clean. Leave to cool in the tin.

3 Release the cake from the tin and use a 6 cm (2½ inch) heart-shaped biscuit cutter to cut out 7 or 8 hearts.

2 bananas, mashed

150 g (5 oz) dairy-free margarine

150 ml (¼ pint) agave nectar

3 large free-range eggs

150 g (5 oz) sultanas

100 g (3½ oz) ground almonds

100 g (3½ oz) gluten-free flour mix, sifted

1 teaspoon gluten-free baking powder

1 teaspoon ground cinnamon

Makes 7–8
Baking time 45 minutes

Lemon Drizzle Cake

This simple tangy sponge with its crisp sugar topping is a traditional teatime treat, perfect with a cup of tea on Mother's Day.

200 g (7 oz) butter at room temperature

200 g (7 oz) golden caster sugar

3 large free-range eggs

200 g (7 oz) self-raising flour, sifted

Grated rind of 1 lemon

Lemon drizzle

Juice of 1½ lemons

125 g (4 oz) golden caster sugar

Serves 8–10
Baking time 50 minutes

1 Preheat the oven to 180°C (350°F), Gas Mark 4, and grease and lightly flour a loaf tin, approximately 10 cm (4 inches) wide and 20 cm (8 inches) long.

2 Lightly cream the butter until light and fluffy, then beat in the caster sugar until just combined. Beat in the eggs one at a time. Gently fold in the flour, taking care not to overwork the mixture, then fold in the lemon rind. Spoon the mixture into the prepared tin, level the surface and cook in the preheated oven for 50 minutes until a skewer inserted into the cake comes out clean.

3 Leave the cake to cool in the tin for about 30 minutes, then use a fork to make holes all over the top of the cake. Mix the lemon juice and caster sugar to make the drizzle, then pour evenly over the cake in the tin. When completely cool, remove the cake from the tin, slice and serve.

Classic Coffee Cake

Our coffee cake is extremely popular, particularly on Sundays! My granny used to make coffee cake for Sunday tea and I never liked it, but I do now, so it's definitely a cake for adults.

250 g (8 oz) butter at room temperature

225 g (7½ oz) golden caster sugar

4 large free-range eggs

2 teaspoons vanilla essence

2 tablespoons instant coffee granules

250 g (8 oz) self-raising flour, sifted

Coffee buttercream

500 g (1 lb) icing sugar, sifted

100 g (3½ oz) butter at room temperature

1 teaspoon vanilla essence

50 ml (2 fl oz) strong coffee

To decorate

White chocolate buttons

Milk chocolate chips

Chocolate strand sprinkles

Serves 8–10

Baking time 25 minutes

1 Preheat the oven to 180°C (350°F), Gas Mark 4, and grease and line the bottoms of two 20 cm (8 inch) loose-bottomed cake tins. Lightly cream the butter until smooth and fluffy, then beat in the caster sugar until just combined. Beat in the eggs one at a time, followed by the vanilla essence. Gently fold in the coffee granules and flour, taking care not to overwork the mixture.

2 Divide the mixture between the tins, level the surface with a spoon and cook for 25 minutes until the tops are golden and a skewer inserted into the cakes comes out clean. Leave the cakes to cool before releasing them from the tins.

3 To make the buttercream, place the icing sugar in a large mixing bowl and beat in the butter and vanilla essence. Slowly add the coffee to make a smooth, creamy icing. Use half the buttercream to sandwich the cakes together and leave to set for 30 minutes.

4 Use a flat spatula to spread the remaining icing on top of the cake, then alternate white chocolate buttons and chocolate chips in a circle around the edge. Sprinkle the centre of the cake with chocolate chips and chocolate strand sprinkles.

Apple and Date Cake

This great cake is suitable for those with food intolerances and type 2 diabetics alike. It contains no sugar, but is sweetened with apples and dates.

1 Preheat the oven to 180°C (350°F), Gas Mark 4, and grease and line the bottom of a 23 cm (9 inch) loose-bottomed cake tin. Blend the apples and dates in a food processor until finely blended and well combined.

2 Transfer the fruits to a mixing bowl and beat in the margarine. Beat in the eggs one at a time, then fold in the ground almonds. Gently fold in the flour, baking powder and cinnamon until well combined, taking care not to overwork the mixture.

3 Transfer the mixture to the prepared tin and cook in the preheated oven for 45 minutes until the top begins to brown and a skewer inserted into the cake comes out clean. Leave to cool in the tin, then release and serve in slices.

300 g (10 oz) apples, peeled, cored and chopped

150 g (5 oz) dates, chopped

150 g (5 oz) dairy-free margarine

3 large free-range eggs

75 g (3 oz) ground almonds

75 g (3 oz) gluten-free flour mix, sifted

1 teaspoon gluten-free baking powder

1½ teaspoons ground cinnamon

Serves 8–10
Baking time 45 minutes

Light Hazelnut Cake

This flour-free sponge is light and airy, with a delightfully nutty flavour complemented by a hint of coffee.

200 g (7 oz) whole blanched hazelnuts

4 large free-range eggs, separated

150 g (5 oz) golden caster sugar

1 teaspoon instant coffee granules

Icing sugar, for dusting

Serves 8
Baking time 35 minutes

1 Preheat the oven to 180°C (350°F), Gas Mark 4, and grease and line the bottom of a 20 cm (8 inch) loose-bottomed cake tin. Blitz the hazelnuts in a food processor until they are finely ground.

2 Beat the egg yolks with the caster sugar and coffee granules, then mix with the ground hazelnuts to form a stiff paste. Whisk the egg whites until they form soft peaks. Gently fold the egg whites, a quarter at a time, into the hazelnut mixture, taking care not to stir or beat to retain the air and keep the cake light.

3 Transfer the mixture to the prepared cake tin and cook in the preheated oven for 35 minutes until golden. Cool in the tin, then release, dust with icing sugar and serve in slices.

Vegan Chocolate and Nut Cake

This delicious chocolate cake has a pleasing crunch from the hazelnuts. You can also make this recipe without the nuts if you prefer.

1 Preheat the oven to 180°C (350°F), Gas Mark 4, and grease and line the bottoms of two 20 cm (8 inch) loose-bottomed cake tins. Mix the flour, baking powder, cocoa and caster sugar in a large mixing bowl. Beat in the vanilla essence, measured water and sunflower oil, then fold in the chopped hazelnuts until well combined.

2 Divide the mixture between the prepared tins and cook for 45 minutes until a skewer inserted into the cakes comes out clean. Leave the cakes to cool before releasing them from the tins.

3 To make the icing, place the icing sugar and cocoa in a large mixing bowl and beat in the margarine and hazelnut syrup. Add the measured water slowly to combine. Use half the icing to sandwich the cakes together and leave to set for 30 minutes.

4 Use a palette knife to spread the remaining icing over the top of the cake and decorate with whole hazelnuts and chocolate chips.

400 g (13 oz) self-raising flour, sifted

3 teaspoons baking powder

75 g (3 oz) cocoa powder, sifted

400 g (13 oz) golden caster sugar

2 teaspoons vanilla essence

450 ml (¾ pint) water

185 ml (6½ fl oz) sunflower oil

150 g (5 oz) hazelnuts, roughly chopped

Chocolate hazelnut icing

500 g (1 lb) icing sugar, sifted

50 g (2 oz) cocoa powder, sifted

75 g (3 oz) dairy-free margarine

2 teaspoons hazelnut syrup

75 ml (3 fl oz) water

To decorate

Whole skin-on hazelnuts

Vegan chocolate chips

Serves 8–10
Cooking time 45 minutes

Chocolate Chip Tray Bake

This quick and easy tray bake uses a vanilla sponge to avoid overdoing the chocolate – but it's packed with chocolatey goodness inside.

250 g (8 oz) butter at room temperature

250 g (8 oz) golden caster sugar

4 large free-range eggs

1 teaspoon vanilla essence

250 g (8 oz) self-raising flour, sifted

2 teaspoons baking powder

75 g (3 oz) milk chocolate chips

75 g (3 oz) white chocolate chips

100 g (3½ oz) sugar-coated chocolate drops or Smarties

4 chocolate digestive biscuits, crushed

Makes 12 large pieces
Baking time 45 minutes

1 Preheat the oven to 180°C (350°F), Gas Mark 4, and grease and line the bottom of a shallow baking tray, approximately 33 x 23 cm (13 x 9 inches).

2 Lightly cream the butter until smooth and fluffy, then beat in the sugar until just combined. Beat in the eggs one at a time, followed by the vanilla essence. Gently fold in the flour and baking powder, taking care not to overwork the mixture.

3 Stir the remaining ingredients into the cake mixture, pour into the prepared tin and level the surface. Cook in the preheated oven for 45 minutes until golden. Leave to cool in the tray, then slice and serve straight from the tray.

Earl Grey Cupcakes

With the subtle flavour of bergamot orange from the Earl Grey tea, these pretty cupcakes make a special treat for Mother's Day.

1 Heat the double cream gently in a small saucepan over a low heat, add the tea bags and keep stirring, taking care not to break the bags. Take off the heat and leave to soak for 30 minutes, then remove the tea bags and discard.

2 Preheat the oven to 200°C (400°F), Gas Mark 6, and line a 12-hole muffin tray with paper cases. Lightly cream the butter until light and fluffy, then beat in the caster sugar until just combined. Beat in the eggs one at a time. Gently fold in the flour, followed by the cream mixture. Divide the mixture between the paper cases and cook in the preheated oven for 20 minutes until golden. Leave to cool in the tray.

3 To make the buttercream, place the icing sugar in a large mixing bowl, beat in the butter, then add the tea slowly to combine. Add the blue colouring carefully to reach the desired colour. Ice the tops of the cakes using the back of a teaspoon, top with the sugar flowers and dust with glitter.

200 ml (7 fl oz) double cream

3 Earl Grey tea bags

50 g (2 oz) butter at room temperature

150 g (5 oz) golden caster sugar

2 large free-range eggs

150 g (5 oz) self-raising flour, sifted

Earl Grey buttercream

500 g (1 lb) icing sugar, sifted

100 g (3½ oz) butter at room temperature

50 ml (2 fl oz) Earl Grey tea, cooled

Blue food colouring

To decorate

Sugar flowers

Edible blue glitter

Makes 12
Baking time 20 minutes

Simnel Cake

This traditional Easter cake is topped with marzipan balls to represent the apostles. Simnel cake is a lighter version of a classic fruit cake.

Icing sugar, for dusting

150 g (5 oz) white marzipan

200 g (7 oz) butter at room temperature

175 g (6 oz) golden caster sugar

3 large free-range eggs, beaten

250 g (8 oz) plain flour, sifted

1½ teaspoons ground cinnamon

½ teaspoon ground nutmeg

250 g (8 oz) currants

200 g (7 oz) sultanas

75 g (3 oz) mixed candied peel

2 tablespoons milk

Topping

250 g (8 oz) golden marzipan

3 tablespoons apricot jam, sieved and warmed

Serves 8–10
Baking time 4 hours

1 Preheat the oven to 160°C (325°F), Gas Mark 3, and grease and line the bottom and sides of a 20 cm (8 inch) loose-bottomed cake tin. Dust a work surface with icing sugar and roll out the white marzipan into a 20 cm (8 inch) disc and set aside.

2 Cream together the butter and caster sugar until smooth and creamy, then beat in the eggs one-third at a time. Fold in the flour, spices and fruit until well combined, then add the milk to loosen the batter a little. Pour half the mixture into the prepared cake tin and level the surface. Place the marzipan disc over the top, then pour the rest of the batter into the tin and level again.

3 Cook in the preheated oven for 1 hour, then lower the temperature to 150°C (300°F), Gas Mark 2, and continue cooking for another 3 hours until the cake is a dark golden colour and a skewer inserted into the cake comes out clean. Leave the cake to cool in the tin.

4 Release the cake from the tin and prepare the topping. Dust a work surface with icing sugar and roll out about two-thirds of the golden marzipan into a disc large enough to blanket the cake. Brush the cake all over with the warmed jam and then smooth the marzipan in place to cover the whole cake. Use the remaining marzipan to make 12 small balls and space them around the edges of the cake, securing with a little apricot jam.

Chocolate Mint Cupcakes

I love the combination of mint and chocolate in these dairy- and gluten-free cakes. The light chocolate sponge is topped with lashings of luscious mint icing.

1. Preheat the oven to 200°C (400°F), Gas Mark 6, and line a 12-hole muffin tray with paper cases. Lightly cream the margarine until light and fluffy, then beat in the caster sugar until just combined. Beat in the eggs one at a time, followed by the vanilla essence. Gently fold in the flour, baking powder and cocoa, taking care not to overwork the mixture.

2. Divide the mixture between the paper cases and cook in the preheated oven for 20 minutes. Leave to cool in the tray.

3. To make the icing, place the icing sugar in a large mixing bowl and beat in the margarine. Slowly add the measured water and peppermint essence to make a smooth, creamy icing, then colour with a little green food colouring. Add a drop at a time until you achieve your desired colour.

4. Use the back of a teaspoon to spread the icing over the tops of the cakes, then sprinkle with grated chocolate.

150 g (5 oz) dairy-free margarine

150 g (5 oz) golden caster sugar

2 large free-range eggs

1 teaspoon gluten-free vanilla essence

125 g (4 oz) rice flour, sifted

1 teaspoon gluten-free baking powder

50 g (2 oz) cocoa powder, sifted

1–2 squares of dairy-free plain dark chocolate, finely grated

Mint icing

500 g (1 lb) icing sugar, sifted

50 g (2 oz) dairy-free margarine

50 ml (2 fl oz) water

1 tablespoon peppermint essence

Green food colouring

Makes 12
Baking time 20 minutes

Easter Bunny Biscuits

The perfect alternative to chocolate treats for Easter and great to make with the kids, these adorable bunnies are ideal for an Easter egg hunt, an Easter tea or as Easter gifts for family and friends.

200 g (7 oz) salted butter at room temperature

175 g (6 oz) golden caster sugar

1 large free-range egg

1 teaspoon vanilla essence

425 g (14 oz) plain flour, sifted, plus extra for dusting

Makes 50
Baking time 10 minutes

1 Cream the butter until light and fluffy, then gently beat in the sugar until just combined. Beat in the egg and the vanilla essence, then mix in the flour until you have a soft dough. Form into a ball, wrap in clingfilm and chill for at least 2 hours.

2 Preheat the oven to 180°C (350°F), Gas Mark 4, and cover two baking sheets with baking parchment. Lightly dust a work surface with flour and roll out the dough to approximately 4 mm (¼ inch) thick. Use a bunny-shaped cutter to cut out the biscuits and carefully lift them onto the prepared baking sheets using a spatula. Bake for 10 minutes until lightly golden at the edges. Allow to cool on the trays.

Kimberley's Cappuccino Cakes

These cupcakes are named after my friend because they were always her favourite. They look like real cappuccinos and make a great Father's Day treat.

125 g (4 oz) butter at room temperature

125 g (4 oz) golden caster sugar

2 large free-range eggs

1 teaspoon vanilla essence

125 g (4 oz) self-raising flour, sifted

1 tablespoon instant coffee granules

1 quantity White Chocolate Buttercream (see page 134)

Cocoa powder, for dusting

Makes 12
Baking time 20 minutes

1 Preheat the oven to 200°C (400°F), Gas Mark 6, and line a 12-hole muffin tray with paper cases. Lightly cream the butter until light and fluffy, then beat in the sugar until just combined. Beat in the eggs one at a time, followed by the vanilla essence. Gently fold in the flour and coffee granules, taking care not to overwork the mixture.

2 Divide the mixture between the paper cases and cook in the preheated oven for 20 minutes. Leave to cool in the tray.

3 Use the back of a teaspoon to spread the buttercream over the tops of the cakes, then sieve a dusting of cocoa on top.

Vegan Banana Cake

This deliciously moist cake is free from dairy and eggs, suitable for vegans and the lactose intolerant. The combination of banana and peanut butter is sublime.

1 Preheat the oven to 180°C (350°F), Gas Mark 4, and grease and line the bottoms of two 20 cm (8 inch) loose-bottomed cake tins. Place the flour in a large mixing bowl and stir in the baking powder and caster sugar. Beat in the sunflower oil, measured water and vanilla essence, then fold in the mashed bananas until well combined.

2 Divide the mixture between the prepared tins and cook in the preheated oven for 45 minutes until a skewer inserted into the cakes comes out clean. Leave the cakes to cool before releasing them from the tins.

3 To make the icing, place the icing sugar in a large mixing bowl and beat in the margarine and peanut butter. Slowly add the measured water to make a smooth icing. Use half the icing to sandwich the cakes together, then leave to set for 30 minutes.

4 Use a palette knife to smooth the remaining icing over the top of the cake and decorate with banana chips.

450 g (14½ oz) self-raising flour, sifted

3 teaspoons baking powder

400 g (13 oz) golden caster sugar

185 ml (6½ fl oz) sunflower oil

450 ml (¾ pint) water

2 teaspoons vanilla essence

2 large ripe bananas, mashed

Dried banana chips, to decorate

Peanut butter icing

500 g (1 lb) icing sugar, sifted

65 g (2½ oz) dairy-free margarine

150 g (5 oz) smooth peanut butter

50 ml (2 fl oz) water

Serves 8–10
Baking time 45 minutes

High summer

Summer is the season when people are watching their weight to look fabulous in their bikinis, but it is also a time when you can enjoy being outside with family and friends. There are so many delicious fruits and berries in season at this time of year that you really should take advantage. Have friends round for tea and cakes in the garden, or make a delicious Midsummer Strawberry Cake, filled with fresh cream and strawberries and lashings of strawberry icing, as dessert for a dinner party al fresco. Friends will love you if you take homemade cakes along to a barbecue or picnic: Juicy Blueberry Muffins and Summer Fruit Cupcakes are perfect for this.

Summer Tea Menu

♥

Finger sandwiches (see page 10)

Exotic Fruit Scones (see page 15)

Midsummer Strawberry Cake
(see page 84)

Summer Fruit Cupcakes (see page 83)

Juicy Blueberry Muffins (see page 82)

Berry Crumble Slices (see page 80)

Halloween

Even though Halloween is about ghoulish, scary things, to me it is always great fun and a chance to celebrate the fabulous seasonal flavours. During the dark chill of autumn, the warming taste of cinnamon, the bright glow of oranges and pumpkins and the juiciness of warm apple can bring great comfort.

The pumpkin recipes included here offer a great way to use up the flesh of Halloween pumpkins and taste absolutely delicious. Get into the spirit of Halloween by dressing up, having a giggle and making some of these treats with friends and family.

Halloween Suggestions

♥

Cat- and bat-shaped biscuits (see Easter Bunny Biscuits, page 74)

Party Popcorn Buckets (see page 32)

Pumpkin Cupcakes (see page 86)

Apple Crumble (see page 87)

Pumpkin and Chocolate Slices (see page 90)

Carrot Cake (see page 88)

Festival of lights

Like Halloween, fireworks in the autumn make everything seem so much brighter, whether you are celebrating Diwali or Bonfire Night. Seeing the dark night sky lit up with colourful sparkles and twinkles gives you a magical feeling. It can be very cold outside, so warming up with delicious treats and soothing hot chocolate is essential. The recipes I have created here can be enjoyed with the family at home or shared with friends at fireworks parties. The Red Velvet Sparkler Cake and the Bollywood Vegan Cupcakes incorporate the bright colours of the season and the sparklers on the Red Velvet Sparkler Cake make it really spectacular for a party.

Fireworks Party Suggestions

♥

Star-shaped sandwiches (see page 10)

Bollywood Vegan Cupcakes (see page 92)

Red Velvet Sparkler Cake (see page 94)

Zesty Orange Cupcakes (see page 91)

Creamy Hot Chocolate (see page 96)

Christmas

Christmas is a really special time of year, one for sharing and giving. I like to include everyone at Christmas, so I have devised recipes for Christmas cakes that are free from gluten, dairy products, eggs and sugar, as well as the traditional 'full of everything' Christmas cake. I also offer alternative cake recipes, which still follow the flavours of the season, for those who simply don't like fruit cake. The Christmas period is the ultimate time for indulgence, a time when many of us allow ourselves unlimited treats – and so we should, we deserve it! It's a great time to enjoy baking, at home alone or with the children, or creating fabulous treats to share with friends and family or to give as gifts.

Christmas Suggestions

♥

Star- or holly-shaped sandwiches (see page 10)

Christmas Cake (see pages 98, 100 and 101)

Irish Cream Cupcakes (see page 97)

Orange and Cranberry Muffins (see page 106)

Brandy Snap Cake (see page 108)

Festive Gingerbread Cakes (see page 105)

Berry Crumble Slices

These crumble slices combine two of my favourite things – cake and crumble!
You could use other seasonal fruits such as apples and pears in autumn.

250 g (8 oz) chilled butter

250 g (8 oz) golden caster sugar

4 large free-range eggs

1 teaspoon vanilla essence

250 g (8 oz) self-raising flour, sifted

2 teaspoons baking powder

250 g (8 oz) strawberries and raspberries, chopped

Crumble topping

250 g (8 oz) self-raising flour, sifted

125 g (4 oz) chilled butter, cubed

125 g (4 oz) golden caster sugar

Makes 12
Baking time 45 minutes

1 Preheat the oven to 180°C (350°F), Gas Mark 4, and grease and line the bottom of a shallow baking tray, approximately 33 x 23 cm (13 x 9 inches). Prepare the crumble by placing the flour in a large mixing bowl and rubbing in the butter with your fingertips until the mixture resembles breadcrumbs of your chosen consistency. I like to have a few big lumps for extra crunch. Mix in the caster sugar with your hands.

2 To make the cake base, lightly cream the butter until light and fluffy, then beat in the caster sugar until just combined. Beat in the eggs one at a time, followed by the vanilla essence. Gently fold in the flour and baking powder until well combined. Transfer the mixture to the baking tray and spread out evenly.

3 Scatter the fruit lightly on top of the cake mixture, then top with the crumble. Bake in the preheated oven for 45 minutes until the topping is golden. Leave to cool in the tray, then slice and serve straight from the tray.

Juicy Blueberry Muffins

This is a classic recipe for milky muffins, packed with juicy blueberries. These muffins are always popular because they are not too sweet.

75 g (3 oz) butter, melted
1 teaspoon vanilla essence
150 ml (¼ pint) whole milk
2 large free-range eggs, beaten
200 g (7 oz) self-raising flour, sifted
125 g (4 oz) golden caster sugar
150 g (5 oz) blueberries

Makes 12
Baking time 20 minutes

1 Preheat the oven to 200°C (400°F), Gas Mark 6, and line a 12-hole muffin tray with paper cases. Place the melted butter in a large mixing bowl and whisk in the vanilla essence and milk, then beat in the eggs.

2 Mix the flour and sugar in a separate bowl, then gently fold into the milk mixture one-third at a time. Fold in the blueberries until evenly distributed.

3 Divide the mixture between the paper cases and cook in the preheated oven for 20 minutes until a skewer inserted into the muffins comes out clean. Serve warm.

Summer Fruit Cupcakes

With delicious, light, gluten-free sponge topped with lashings of dairy-free buttercream and succulent fresh fruit, these are the perfect summertime treat.

1. Preheat the oven to 200°C (400°F), Gas Mark 6, and line a 12-hole muffin tray with paper cases. Lightly cream the margarine until light and fluffy, then beat in the caster sugar until just combined. Beat in the eggs one at a time, followed by the vanilla essence. Gently fold in the flour and baking powder, taking care not to overwork the mixture, then fold in the chopped fruits until evenly distributed.

2. Divide the mixture between the paper cases and cook in the preheated oven for 20–25 minutes until a skewer inserted into the cakes comes out clean. Leave to cool in the tray.

3. To make the buttercream, place the icing sugar in a large mixing bowl and beat in the margarine. Slowly add the orange juice and vanilla essence to make a smooth, creamy icing. Use the back of a teaspoon to spread the icing over the tops of the cakes. Top each cake with a raspberry, a strawberry and a blueberry, arranged in a cluster in the centre.

150 g (5 oz) dairy-free margarine

150 g (5 oz) golden caster sugar

2 large free-range eggs

1 teaspoon gluten-free vanilla essence

150 g (5 oz) rice flour, sifted

1 teaspoon gluten-free baking powder

8 raspberries, quartered

12 blueberries, halved

4 strawberries, finely chopped

Dairy-free buttercream

500 g (1 lb) icing sugar, sifted

50 g (2 oz) dairy-free margarine

50 ml (2 fl oz) orange juice

½ teaspoon gluten-free vanilla essence

To decorate

12 raspberries

12 strawberries

12 blueberries

Makes 12
Baking time 20–25 minutes

Midsummer Strawberry Cake

This is a sumptuous cake for a summer tea party in the garden. Filled with fresh cream and strawberries, it is an indulgent treat for summer holiday guests.

250 g (8 oz) butter at room temperature

225 g (7½ oz) golden caster sugar

4 large free-range eggs

275 g (9 oz) self-raising flour, sifted

150 g (5 oz) strawberries, roughly chopped

Filling

6 large strawberries

200 ml (7 fl oz) double cream, whipped

Strawberry buttercream

250 g (8 oz) icing sugar, sifted

50 g (2 oz) butter at room temperature

1 teaspoon natural strawberry flavouring

25 ml (1 fl oz) water

To decorate

10 large whole strawberries

Jumbo heart sprinkles

Serves 8–10

Baking time 25–30 minutes

1 Preheat the oven to 180°C (350°F), Gas Mark 4, and grease and line two 20 cm (8 inch) loose-bottomed cake tins. Lightly cream the butter until light and fluffy, then beat in the caster sugar until just combined. Beat in the eggs one at a time. Gently fold in the flour, taking care not to overwork the mixture and then fold in the chopped strawberries until evenly distributed.

2 Divide the mixture between the tins and cook in the preheated oven for 25–30 minutes until a skewer inserted into the cakes comes out clean. Leave to cool in the tins.

3 To make the filling, crush the strawberries with a fork and fold into the whipped cream. To make the buttercream, place the icing sugar in a large mixing bowl and beat in the butter and strawberry flavouring. Add the water slowly to combine.

4 Once the cakes have cooled completely, release from the tins and sandwich together with the filling. Set aside for 30 minutes, then spread the top of the cake with strawberry buttercream and top with whole strawberries and jumbo heart sprinkles.

Pumpkin Cupcakes

Perfect to get you into the festive spirit at a Halloween party, these tasty cupcakes can be made from the pumpkin flesh leftover from your Halloween lantern, and look great with spooky decorations.

125 g (4 oz) butter at room temperature

150 g (5 oz) golden caster sugar

2 large free-range eggs

1 tablespoon runny honey

175 g (6 oz) cooked mashed pumpkin

175 g (6 oz) self-raising flour, sifted

1 teaspoon ground cinnamon, plus extra for dusting

1 quantity Cream Cheese Icing (see page 94)

Makes 12
Baking time 20 minutes

1 Preheat the oven to 200°C (400°F), Gas Mark 6, and line a 12-hole muffin tray with paper cases. Lightly cream the butter until light and fluffy, then beat in the caster sugar until just combined. Beat in the eggs one at a time, followed by the honey and the pumpkin. Gently fold in the flour and cinnamon, taking care not to overwork the mixture.

2 Divide the mixture between the paper cases and cook in the preheated oven for 20 minutes. Leave to cool in the tray.

3 Use the back of a teaspoon to spread the icing over the tops of the cakes, then sieve a dusting of cinnamon on top.

Apple Crumble

Apple crumble is an all-time favourite and very simple to make. Serve warm
on a chilly autumn day with lashings of cream or custard.

1 Preheat the oven to 160°C (325°F), Gas Mark 3, and grease
a shallow ovenproof dish or tin approximately 30 x 20 cm
(12 x 8 inches).

2 Place the apples in a saucepan with just enough boiling water
to cover them, add the caster sugar and stir. Bring to the boil
and simmer over a medium heat until the apples soften a
little. Drain off the excess liquid and spread out in the bottom
of the dish or tin. Sprinkle with the demerara sugar and
cinnamon.

3 Prepare the crumble by placing the flour in a large mixing
bowl and rubbing in the butter with your fingertips until the
mixture resembles breadcrumbs of your chosen consistency.
I like to have a few big lumps for extra crunch. Mix in the
sugar with your hands.

4 Scatter the crumble evenly over the apples and bake for
35 minutes until the topping is golden. Leave to cool for
at least 30 minutes before serving warm with single cream
or custard.

500 g (1 lb) cooking apples, peeled,
    cored and sliced
75 g (3 oz) golden caster sugar
1 tablespoon demerara sugar
2 teaspoons ground cinnamon
single cream or custard, to serve

Crumble topping
325 g (11 oz) plain flour
175 g (6 oz) chilled butter, cubed
175 g (6 oz) golden caster sugar

Serves 8–10
Baking time 35 minutes

Carrot Cake

This classic cake is moist and full of flavour, and made with sunflower oil, which is a little healthier than butter. Follow the tips below to make a dairy- and gluten-free version.

150 ml (¼ pint) sunflower oil

150 g (5 oz) light muscovado sugar

2 large free-range eggs

200 g (7 oz) self-raising flour, sifted

2 teaspoons ground mixed spice

1 teaspoon ground cinnamon

100 g (3½ oz) sultanas

75 g (3 oz) desiccated coconut

75 g (3 oz) pecan nuts, roughly chopped

175 g (6 oz) grated carrot

½ quantity Cream Cheese Icing (see page 94)

Serves 8–10
Baking time 1¾ hours

1 Preheat the oven to 150°C (300°F), Gas Mark 2, and grease and line the bottom of a deep 20 cm (8 inch) loose-bottomed cake tin.

2 Beat the sunflower oil with the sugar until well combined, then beat in the eggs one at a time and fold in the flour, mixed spice and cinnamon until just combined. Fold in the sultanas, coconut, pecans and carrot until evenly distributed through the mixture.

3 Spoon the mixture into the prepared tin and cook in the preheated oven for 1¾ hours until a skewer inserted into the cake comes out clean. Leave the cake to cool before releasing from the tin. When completely cooled, swirl the Cream Cheese Icing over the top of the cake.

♥ **Tip:** *The sponge uses sunflower oil, so top it with ½ quantity of Dairy-free Buttercream (see page 20) to make the whole cake free from dairy products. If you want to make it gluten-free too, replace the self-raising flour with the same quantity of rice flour and 2 teaspoons of gluten-free baking powder.* ♥

Pumpkin and Chocolate Slices

These melt-in-the-mouth slices are delicious. Even I don't like the idea of pumpkin in a cake, but trust me – it makes these so moist and gooey.

200 g (7 oz) butter at room temperature

175 g (6 oz) golden caster sugar

3 tablespoons maple syrup

4 large free-range eggs

300 g (10 oz) cooked mashed pumpkin

250 g (8 oz) self-raising flour, sifted

1 teaspoon ground cinnamon

25 g (1 oz) cocoa powder, sifted

125 g (4 oz) chocolate chips

Makes 15
Baking time 35–40 minutes

1   Preheat the oven to 180°C (350°F), Gas Mark 4, and grease and line the bottom of a shallow baking tray, approximately 33 x 23 cm (13 x 9 inches). Lightly cream the butter until light and fluffy, then beat in the sugar and maple syrup until just combined.

2   Beat in the eggs one at a time, followed by the pumpkin. Sift together the flour, cinnamon and cocoa, then gently fold into the mixture, taking care not to overwork.

3   Fold in the chocolate chips, then transfer the mixture to the prepared tin and cook in the preheated oven for 35–40 minutes until golden. Leave to cool in the tray, then slice and serve straight from the tray.

Zesty Orange Cupcakes

These orange cupcakes have a light, refreshing citrus flavour and are suitable for coeliacs and those who suffer from gluten or dairy intolerances.

1 Preheat the oven to 200°C (400°F), Gas Mark 6, and line a 12-hole muffin tray with paper cases. Lightly cream the margarine until light and fluffy, then beat in the caster sugar until just combined. Beat in the eggs one at a time, followed by the vanilla essence. Gently fold in the flour and baking powder, taking care not to overwork the mixture, then fold in the grated orange rind until evenly distributed.

2 Divide the mixture between the paper cases and cook in the preheated oven for 20 minutes until a skewer inserted into the cakes comes out clean. Leave to cool in the tray.

3 To make the icing, place the icing sugar in a large mixing bowl and beat in the margarine. Slowly add the orange juice and grated rind to make a smooth, creamy icing. Use the back of a teaspoon to spread the icing over the tops of the cakes.

4 Dust a work surface with icing sugar and roll out the fondant icing. Use flower-shaped biscuit cutters to cut out 12 large and 12 small flowers. Place a large flower on top of each cake, then position a small flower on top. Use the writing icing to pipe a small dot in the centre of each double flower.

150 g (5 oz) dairy-free margarine

150 g (5 oz) golden caster sugar

2 large free-range eggs

1 teaspoon gluten-free vanilla essence

150 g (5 oz) rice flour, sifted

1 teaspoon gluten-free baking powder

Grated rind of ½ large orange

100 g (3½ oz) orange ready-to-roll fondant icing

Yellow writing icing tube (free from dairy and gluten)

Orange icing

500 g (1 lb) icing sugar, sifted, plus extra for dusting

50 g (2 oz) dairy-free margarine

50 ml (2 fl oz) orange juice

Grated rind of ½ large orange

Makes 12
Baking time 20 minutes

Bollywood Vegan Cupcakes

These vibrant cupcakes were designed for Diwali, the festival of lights, celebrated by Hindus, Sikhs and Jains all over the world. The eggless mixture is perfect for vegans.

300 g (10 oz) self-raising flour, sifted

1 teaspoon baking powder

250 g (8 oz) golden caster sugar

2 teaspoons vanilla essence

125 ml (4 fl oz) sunflower oil

300 ml (½ pint) water

Glacé icing

450 g (14½ oz) icing sugar, sifted

50 ml (2 fl oz) water

Red and blue food colourings

To decorate

Edible sugar roses and leaves

Writing icing tube

Edible gold paint

Edible gold glitter

Makes 20

Baking time 20 minutes

1 Preheat the oven to 200°C (400°F), Gas Mark 6, and line two muffin trays with 20 gold paper cases. Place the flour in a large mixing bowl and mix in the baking powder, the sugar, then the vanilla essence. Beat in the sunflower oil and water slowly to combine.

2 Divide the runny mixture between the paper cases using a small spoon, or transfer to a small jug and pour it in. Cook in the preheated oven for 20 minutes until a skewer inserted into the cakes comes out clean. Leave to cool in the trays.

3 To make the icing, place the icing sugar in a large mixing bowl and stir in the water. Divide between two bowls and colour one batch red and the other blue. Use the back of a teaspoon to ice the cupcakes.

4 Decorate the cakes with roses and leaves, then use the writing icing to pipe paisley motifs. Use a small paintbrush and edible paint to colour the paisley motifs gold, then sprinkle with edible gold glitter.

Red Velvet Sparkler Cake

Perfect for Bonfire Night, this rich, moist cake contains both vanilla and a small amount of cocoa. The distinctive colour is achieved by adding red food colouring to the sponge.

300 g (10 oz) butter at room temperature

300 g (10 oz) caster sugar

3 large free-range eggs

1 teaspoon vanilla essence

2 teaspoons red food colouring

200 ml (7 fl oz) buttermilk

300 g (10 oz) self-raising flour, sifted

1 teaspoon cocoa powder, sifted

2 teaspoons baking powder

Cream cheese icing

500 g (1 lb) icing sugar, sifted

50 g (2 oz) butter at room temperature

100 g (3½ oz) cream cheese

50 ml (2 fl oz) water

To decorate

Edible gold star sugar decorations

Edible gold star glitter

Indoor star sparklers

Serves 8–10

Baking time 40 minutes

1　Preheat the oven to 180°C (350°F), Gas Mark 4, and grease and line the bottoms of two deep 20 cm (8 inch) loose-bottomed cake tins.

2　Lightly cream the butter until light and fluffy, then beat in the caster sugar until just combined. Beat in the eggs one at a time, followed by the vanilla essence and red food colouring. Gently fold in the buttermilk, taking care not to overwork the mixture, then fold in the flour, cocoa and baking powder until just combined.

3　Divide the mixture between the tins and cook in the preheated oven for 40 minutes until a skewer inserted into the cakes comes out clean. Leave the cakes to cool before releasing from the tins.

4　Prepare the icing by mixing the icing sugar, butter and cream cheese in a large mixing bowl, then gradually adding the water a little at a time. Sandwich the cakes together with a small amount of the icing, then leave to set for 30 minutes. Use a flat spatula to cover the top and sides of the cake with the remaining icing, then decorate with gold stars, glitter and sparklers.

Creamy Hot Chocolate

This creamy hot chocolate, provides the perfect way to warm up your guests on Bonfire Night.

2 teaspoons granulated sugar

1 heaped teaspoon cocoa powder

100 ml (3½ fl oz) single cream

200 ml (7 fl oz) whole milk

Toppings

Whipped cream

Mini marshmallows

Hundreds and thousands
  sprinkles

Cocoa powder, for dusting

Serves 1

1 Stir the sugar and cocoa together in a large mug, add a dash of boiling water and stir well to make a smooth paste. Combine the single cream and milk in a small saucepan and gently warm over a low heat, stirring continuously, until piping hot.

2 Pour the creamy milk over the chocolate mixture in the mug and stir thoroughly. Top with whipped cream, mini marshmallows, a sprinkling of hundreds and thousands and a dusting of cocoa.

To make Hazelnut Hot Chocolate, replace the sugar with 2 teaspoons of hazelnut syrup.

To make Orange Hot Chocolate, add ½ teaspoon of finely grated orange rind to the cocoa and sugar mixture. Stir in ½ teaspoon of orange essence or 3 teaspoons Cointreau at the end.

To make Mocha, add 1 teaspoon of instant coffee granules to the cocoa and sugar mixture.

To make Irish Cream Hot Chocolate, replace the single cream with Irish Cream liqueur.

Irish Cream Cupcakes

These cupcakes are just divine; a real luxury and one for the ladies. The rich, smooth icing is pure pleasure and will soon get you hooked.

1 Preheat the oven to 200°C (400°F), Gas Mark 6, and line a 12-hole muffin tray with paper cases. Lightly cream the butter until light and fluffy, then beat in the caster sugar until just combined. Beat in the eggs one at a time. Gently fold in the flour and Irish Cream, taking care not to overwork the mixture.

2 Divide the mixture between the paper cases and cook in the preheated oven for 20 minutes until a skewer inserted into the cakes comes out clean. Leave to cool in the tray.

3 To make the icing, place the icing sugar in a large mixing bowl and beat in the butter. Slowly add the Irish Cream and measured water to make a smooth, creamy icing. Use the back of a teaspoon to spread the icing over the tops of the cakes and top each with a single edible gold star.

100 g (3½ oz) butter at room temperature

125 g (4 oz) golden caster sugar

2 large free-range eggs

125 g (4 oz) self-raising flour, sifted

50 ml (2 fl oz) Irish Cream liqueur

12 edible gold star decorations, to decorate

Irish Cream icing

500 g (1 lb) icing sugar, sifted

100 g (3½ oz) butter at room temperature

50 ml (2 fl oz) Irish Cream liqueur

1 tablespoon water

Makes 12
Baking time 20 minutes

Traditional Christmas Cake

This recipe is deliciously moist and very simple to make. It can be made far in advance, leaving the fruit to soak for a least a week, but is just as good made on Christmas Eve.

150 g (5 oz) sultanas
150 g (5 oz) dried cranberries
125 g (4 oz) mixed candied peel
125 g (4 oz) currants
150 g (5 oz) raisins
50 g (2 oz) glacé cherries, chopped
175 ml (6 fl oz) brandy
175 g (6 oz) butter
200 g (7 oz) dark muscovado sugar
50 g (2 oz) black treacle
Grated rind and juice of 1 orange
Grated rind and juice of ½ lemon
300 g (10 oz) unsweetened
   chestnut purée
1 teaspoon ground cinnamon
1 teaspoon ground cloves
1 teaspoon ground nutmeg
½ teaspoon ground ginger
3 large free-range eggs, beaten
250 g (8 oz) self-raising flour, sifted

Serves 8–10
Baking time 2 hours

1 Place all the dried fruits in a plastic container, pour over the brandy and stir well. Cover with a lid and leave to macerate for 1 week.

2 To make the cake, melt the butter in a large saucepan, then stir in the sugar, treacle, orange and lemon rind and juice, chestnut purée and all the spices. Add the soaked fruits and stir over a low heat for 10 minutes, until the chestnut purée has melted. Cover and set aside for 1 hour.

3 Preheat the oven to 150°C (300°F), Gas Mark 2, and grease and line the bottom and sides of a 20 cm (8 inch) loose-bottomed cake tin. Stir the eggs into the fruit mixture, then add the flour and fold in until well combined.

4 Pour the mixture into the prepared tin. Cut a long piece of baking parchment twice the height of the cake tin, wrap around the outside of the tin twice and secure with string. Cook in the preheated oven for 2 hours. Leave to cool in the tin, then release the cake and store in an airtight tub until you are ready to decorate it. See pages 102–4 for decorating ideas.

Vegan Christmas Cake

Slightly fluffier than a traditional Christmas cake, this one contains no eggs or dairy products, bringing good tidings to those with allergies or intolerances.

100 g (3½ oz) sultanas

50 g (2 oz) raisins

75 g (3 oz) mixed candied peel

75 g (3 oz) dried cranberries

25 g (1 oz) currants

100 ml (3½ fl oz) dark rum

250 g (8 oz) dark muscovado sugar

300 g (10 oz) self-raising flour, sifted

2 teaspoons baking powder

2 teaspoons ground cinnamon

1 teaspoon ground nutmeg

½ teaspoon ground cloves

300 ml (½ pint) water

125 ml (4 fl oz) sunflower oil

Grated rind and juice of 1 orange

Grated rind of 1 lemon

Serves 8–10
Baking time 1½–1¾ hours

1 If you have time, soak the fruits in the rum for at least 24 hours for a greater depth of flavour. To do this, mix all the fruits in a bowl, pour over the rum and mix well. Cover and leave for up to 1 week.

2 To make the cake, preheat the oven to 160°C (325°F), Gas Mark 3, and grease and line the bottom of a 20 cm (8 inch) loose-bottomed cake tin. Place the sugar in a large mixing bowl and stir well to remove any lumps. Add the flour, baking powder and spices and stir well.

3 Mix the measured water and sunflower oil in a measuring jug and pour slowly into the dry mixture, stirring continuously, until well combined. Fold in the soaked fruits (or the dried fruits and the rum), the orange rind and juice and the lemon rind and stir well. Transfer the mixture to the prepared tin and cook in the preheated oven for 1½–1¾ hours until a skewer inserted in the cake comes out clean. Leave to cool in the tin, then release the cake and store in an airtight tub until you are ready to decorate it. See pages 102–4 for decorating ideas.

Allergy-friendly Fruit Cake

This cake will make your Christmas if you have to avoid sugar, gluten and dairy products. Moist and packed full of juicy fruits, it is sweetened with agave nectar.

1 Preheat the oven to 160°C (325°F), Gas Mark 3, and grease and line the bottom of a 20 cm (8 inch) loose-bottomed cake tin. Place all the dried fruits into a bowl and use your hands to mix them thoroughly. Set aside.

2 Place the melted margarine and agave nectar into a large mixing bowl and stir to combine. Stir in the eggs, then fold in the dried fruits. Fold in the flour, baking powder, spices and orange rind, then transfer to the prepared tin and cook in the preheated oven for 1½–1¾ hours until a skewer inserted into the cake comes out clean. Leave to cool in the tin, then release the cake and store in an airtight tub.

> ♥ **Tip:** *As this cake is designed to be free from sugar, you cannot decorate it with the traditional icing and marzipan. If you would like to decorate the cake, use the Dried Fruit and Nut Topping on page 102, substituting sugar-free diabetic jam for the apricot jam.* ♥

100 g (3½ oz) sultanas

75 g (3 oz) raisins

75 g (3 oz) sugar-free mixed peel

75 g (3 oz) dried cranberries

25 g (1 oz) currants

50 g (2 oz) dried figs, chopped

250 g (8 oz) dairy-free margarine, melted

250 ml (8 fl oz) agave nectar

3 large free-range eggs, beaten

300 g (10 oz) rice flour, sifted

2 teaspoons gluten-free baking powder

2 teaspoons ground cinnamon

1 teaspoon ground nutmeg

½ teaspoon ground cloves

Grated rind of 1 orange

Serves 8–10
Baking time 1½–1¾ hours

Dried Fruit and Nut Topping

This sumptuous Christmas cake decoration is ideal for those who don't have a sweet tooth and would rather avoid the traditional marzipan and icing. Whole nuts and large chunks of dried fruit are arranged on top of the cake and glazed with apricot jam. Increase the quantities if you want to pile high the mix.

2 tablespoons apricot jam, sieved and warmed

100 g (3½ oz) whole pecan nuts

100 g (3½ oz) blanched almonds

100 g (3½ oz) glacé cherries, halved

100 g (3½ oz) dried figs, halved

100 g (3½ oz) dried dates

Deep gold ribbon

Makes enough to cover a 20 cm (8 inch) cake

1　Use a pastry brush to spread some of the warmed apricot jam over the top of the cake, leaving the sides bare.

2　Arrange the dried fruits and nuts over the top of the cake. Start by arranging a border around the edge of the cake and work your way into the centre making a pattern with the different shapes and textures.

3　Once you have positioned the fruits, glaze the top by brushing more of the jam over them. Make sure that all the gaps between the fruits and nuts have a generous filling of apricot jam. Leave to set overnight. Finish by tying a deep gold ribbon around the sides of the cake and finish with a bow.

♥ **Tip:** *This is the perfect decoration for a sugar-free Christmas cake, such as the Allergy-friendly Fruit Cake (see page 101). However, be sure to use a diabetic apricot jam.* ♥

Basic Cake Icing

This is the starting point for most traditional Christmas cake designs, a layer of marzipan, followed by a smooth layer of icing.

1 Lightly brush the cake all over with warmed apricot jam, covering the top and sides completely.

2 Dust a work surface with icing sugar and roll out the marzipan to a disc large enough to blanket the cake, covering the top and sides. Lay the marzipan over the cake and smooth in place. Trim the edges, leaving about 2 cm (1 inch) of excess marzipan to tuck under the cake.

3 Gently lift the cake and place it upside down on the dusted surface to prevent it sticking. Tuck the loose edges of the marzipan under the cake and neaten all the way round with a knife. Turn the cake back up the right way and place on a cake board. Brush the cake all over again with jam to cover the marzipan.

4 Dust the work surface with icing sugar again and roll out the fondant icing. Use the icing to cover the cake in the same way as the marzipan, tucking the edges all the way round under the cake for a neat finish.

5 Place the cake back onto the cake board, taking care to centre it. The cake is now ready for the decoration of your choice. See page 104 for some ideas.

2 tablespoons apricot jam, sieved and warmed

Icing sugar, for dusting

1 kg (2 lb) white marzipan

1 kg (2 lb) white ready-to-roll fondant icing

Makes enough to cover a 20 cm (8 inch) cake

Snowflake Decoration

Icing sugar, for dusting

100 g (3½ oz) white ready-to-roll
    fondant icing

2 teaspoons apricot jam, sieved
    and warmed

Edible silver balls

Edible silver hologram glitter

Silver ribbon

1 Dust a work surface with icing sugar and roll out the fondant icing. Use a set of snowflake cutters to cut out a number of snowflakes of various sizes. Handling them carefully, lay them on the iced cake to try out different designs.

2 When you have finalized their positions, use a small pastry brush to brush the backs of the snowflakes with jam and stick them to the cake. Use just a tiny amount of jam or it will ooze out the sides.

3 While the icing is still soft, push silver balls into the centres of the snowflakes, then dust the cake with silver glitter. The next day, when the icing has hardened, tie a silver ribbon round the cake.

Holly Decoration

Icing sugar, for dusting

75 g (3 oz) green ready-to-roll
    fondant icing

50 g (2 oz) red ready-to-roll
    fondant icing

2 teaspoons apricot jam, sieved
    and warmed

Edible gold hologram glitter

Red or green ribbon

1 Dust a work surface with icing sugar and roll out the green fondant icing. Use a holly leaf plunge cutter to cut out some leaves. Carefully lay them on the iced cake to try out different designs. I put 3 leaves together in the centre, then pairs of leaves at intervals around the edges of the top of the cake.

2 When you have finalized their positions, use a small pastry brush to brush the backs of the leaves with jam and stick them to the cake. Use just a tiny amount of jam, or it will ooze out the sides.

3 Use the red icing to roll some little berries in your hands and stick them to the cake in the same way, then dust the cake with gold glitter. The next day when the icing has hardened, tie a red or green ribbon round the cake.

Festive Gingerbread Cakes

Dark, spiced sponge, topped with creamy lemon icing, these festive treats are free from gluten and dairy products.

150 g (5 oz) dairy-free margarine

150 g (5 oz) light muscovado sugar

2 large free-range eggs

1 teaspoon gluten-free vanilla essence

150 g (5 oz) rice flour, sifted

1 teaspoon gluten-free baking powder

1 teaspoon ground cinnamon

¼ teaspoon ground cloves

¼ teaspoon ground nutmeg

¼ teaspoon ground ginger

2 teaspoons black treacle

75 g (3 oz) light brown ready-to-roll fondant icing

Lemon buttercream

500 g (1 lb) icing sugar, sifted, plus extra for dusting

50 g (2 oz) diary-free margarine

50 ml (2 fl oz) lemon juice

Makes 12
Baking time 20 minutes

1 Preheat the oven to 200°C (400°F), Gas Mark 6, and line a 12-hole muffin tray with paper cases. Lightly cream the margarine until light and fluffy, then beat in the brown sugar until just combined. Beat in the eggs one at a time, followed by the vanilla essence. Gently fold in the flour, baking powder, spices and treacle, taking care not to overwork the mixture.

2 Divide the mixture between the paper cases and cook in the preheated oven for 20 minutes until a skewer inserted into the cakes comes out clean. Leave to cool in the tray.

3 To make the buttercream, place the icing sugar in a large mixing bowl and beat in the margarine. Slowly add the lemon juice to make a smooth, creamy icing. Use the back of a teaspoon to spread the icing over the tops of the cakes.

4 Dust a work surface with icing sugar and roll out the fondant icing. Use a mini star-shaped plunge cutter to punch out about 60 little stars and arrange them on the tops of the cakes.

Orange and Cranberry Muffins

These dairy- and gluten-free muffins are sure to get you in the mood for Christmas and all things cosy. Perfect as a breakfast treat on Christmas morning or a pick-me-up after a long afternoon Christmas shopping.

175 g (6 oz) dairy-free margarine

150 g (5 oz) light muscovado sugar

3 large free-range eggs

1 teaspoon gluten-free vanilla essence

175 g (6 oz) rice flour, sifted

1 teaspoon gluten-free baking powder

Grated rind of 1 orange

36 fresh cranberries

25 g (1 oz) demerara sugar

½ teaspoon cinnamon

Icing sugar, for dusting (optional)

Makes 12
Baking time 25 minutes

1 Preheat the oven to 200°C (400°F), Gas Mark 6, and line a 12-hole muffin tray with paper cases.

2 Lightly cream the margarine until light and fluffy, then beat in the muscovado sugar until just combined. Beat in the eggs one at a time, followed by the vanilla essence. Gently fold in the rice flour and baking powder, taking care not to overwork the mixture. Lightly fold in the orange rind, then divide the batter among the paper cases.

3 Arrange 3 cranberries on top of each muffin, then mix the demerara sugar and cinnamon in a small bowl and sprinkle over the tops. Bake in the preheated oven for 25 minutes until golden. Serve warm or cold, dusted with icing sugar if you like.

Brandy Snap Cake

This rich, decadent cake is full of festive flavours, but without the dried fruits that some people do not enjoy. This is a great alternative Christmas cake.

200 g (7 oz) butter at room temperature

175 g (6 oz) light muscovado sugar

4 large free-range eggs

50 ml (2 fl oz) milk

1 teaspoon vanilla essence

300 g (10 oz) self-raising flour, sifted

1 teaspoon ground mixed spice

50 g (2 oz) brandy snaps, roughly broken, plus extra to decorate

Gold dragees, to decorate

Brandy butter icing

500 g (1 lb) icing sugar, sifted

1 teaspoon light muscovado sugar

100 g (3½ oz) butter

100 g (3½ oz) cream cheese

5 tablespoons brandy

Serves 8–10
Baking time 30 minutes

1 Preheat the oven to 180°C (350°F), Gas Mark 4, and grease and line the bottoms of two 20 cm (8 inch) loose-bottomed cake tins. Cream the butter until light and fluffy, then beat in the muscovado sugar until just combined. Beat in the eggs one at a time, followed by the milk and vanilla essence.

2 Gently fold in the flour and mixed spice, taking care not to overwork the batter. Fold in the brandy snap pieces, then divide the mixture between the prepared tins, level the surface and cook in the preheated oven for 30 minutes until a skewer inserted into the cakes comes out clean. Leave the cakes to cool before releasing them from the tins.

3 To make the buttercream, place the icing sugar in a large mixing bowl and beat in the muscovado sugar, butter and cream cheese, then add the brandy slowly to combine. Use half the buttercream to sandwich the cakes together and leave to set for 30 minutes.

4 Use a palette knife to spread the remaining icing on top of the cake, then decorate with brandy snaps and gold dragees.

Another Year Older

Chocolate Orange Brownies

The perfect alternative to a traditional birthday cake, these chewy, tangy brownies can be topped with a message and candles. The orange fudge-like topping adds every luxury.

200 g (7 oz) plain dark chocolate

300 g (10 oz) butter

300 g (10 oz) light muscovado sugar

8 free-range eggs, beaten

150 g (5 oz) plain flour

75 g (3 oz) ground almonds

Grated rind of 2 oranges

200 g (7 oz) chocolate chips

Orange fudge topping

350 g (11½ oz) plain dark chocolate

50 ml (2 fl oz) golden syrup

100 g (3½ oz) butter

2 teaspoons orange essence

To decorate

White writing icing tube

Birthday candles

Makes about 28 pieces

Baking time 45–50 minutes

1 Preheat the oven to 180°C (350°F), Gas Mark 4, and grease and line the bottom of a shallow baking tin, approximately 33 x 23 cm (13 x 9 inches). Melt the chocolate and the butter in a heatproof bowl over a saucepan of gently simmering water, stirring regularly. Leave to cool for 10 minutes.

2 Beat in the sugar, then the eggs. Fold in the flour and almonds until well combined, followed by the orange rind and chocolate chips. Transfer the mixture to the prepared tin and level with a spoon. Cook in the preheated oven for 45–50 minutes until the top appears crispy and a skewer inserted into the cake comes out clean. Leave to cool in the tin.

3 To prepare the topping, melt the chocolate, golden syrup and butter in a heatproof bowl over a saucepan of gently simmering water, stirring regularly. Mix in the orange essence and remove from the heat. Leave to cool, then chill for 1 hour to thicken.

4 Remove the brownies from the tin and spread the topping over the surface, smoothing with a palette knife. Leave the topping to set a little, then cut the brownies into enough pieces to spell out your birthday message, one letter per brownie. Arrange the brownies on a large plate, use the writing icing to pipe the message across them, pop the candles into the brownies and serve.

Giant Cupcake

This is a fabulous alternative to a standard birthday cake that makes a spectacular centrepiece at a birthday party. You will need a special baking tin.

375 g (12 oz) butter at room temperature

375 g (12 oz) golden caster sugar

6 large free-range eggs

3 teaspoons vanilla essence

375 g (12 oz) self-raising flour, sifted

Sugar sprinkles, to decorate

Vanilla buttercream

500 g (1 lb) icing sugar, sifted

100 g (3½ oz) butter at room temperature

1 teaspoon vanilla essence

50 ml (2 fl oz) water

Few drops of food colouring

Serves 10
Baking time 1 hour

1 Preheat the oven to 180°C (350°F), Gas Mark 4, and heavily grease your giant cupcake cake tin, taking care to grease in all the corners, especially the tip of the cupcake top.

2 Cream the butter until light and fluffy, then beat in the caster sugar until just combined. Beat in the eggs one at a time, followed by the vanilla essence. Gently fold in the flour, taking care not to overwork the batter. Divide the mixture between the two parts of the tin, with about two-fifths in the top part of the cupcake and three-fifths in the bottom. Cook in the preheated oven for 1 hour until a skewer inserted into the bottom section comes out clean, as this section will take a little longer to cook. Leave to cool in the tin.

3 To make the buttercream, place the icing sugar in a large mixing bowl and beat in the butter and vanilla essence, then add the measured water slowly to make a smooth icing. Add food colouring, a little at a time, until you achieve the desired shade.

4 Once the cake has cooled, carefully release the two sections from the tin. You may have to trim the base of the top part of the cupcake to make it flat enough to stand evenly on the bottom of the cake. Sandwich the parts together using a thin layer of buttercream. Use a palette knife to swirl the remaining buttercream over the cake and top with lots of sprinkles. (see photograph on page 144)

Pretty Petal Cake

Crystallized petals are a little fiddly to prepare but they add a simple elegance to this pretty birthday cake, which will be admired by all.

200 g (7 oz) butter at room temperature

200 g (7 oz) caster sugar

3 large free-range eggs

1 teaspoon vanilla essence

2 tablespoons rose water

300 g (10 oz) self-raising flour, sifted

125 ml (4 fl oz) whole milk

4–5 heaped tablespoons strawberry jam

Orange flower buttercream

275 g (9 oz) icing sugar, sifted

50 g (2 oz) butter at room temperature

2 tablespoons orange flower water

Crystallized petals

20 very fresh rose petals

2 large free-range egg whites at room temperature, lightly beaten

200 g (7 oz) caster sugar

Serves 8–10
Baking time 30 minutes

1 First make the crystallized petals. Rinse the petals in cold water and dry thoroughly on kitchen paper. Cover a baking sheet with baking parchment. Brush the petals with egg white using a small pastry brush, taking care to cover every bit. Dip the petals into the caster sugar until coated on both sides. Shake off any excess sugar, then place on the baking sheet and leave to dry for at least 5 hours in a warm room, or preferably overnight.

2 To make the cake, preheat the oven to 180°C (350°F), Gas Mark 4, and grease and line the bottoms of two 20 cm (8 inch) loose-bottomed cake tins. Lightly cream the butter until light and fluffy, then beat in the caster sugar until just combined. Beat in the eggs one at a time, followed by the vanilla essence and rose water. Gently fold in the flour, taking care not to overwork the mixture, then stir in the milk.

3 Divide the mixture between the tins and bake in the preheated oven for 30 minutes until golden. Leave the cakes to cool before releasing them from the tins.

4 Sandwich the cakes together with strawberry jam and leave to set for 30 minutes. To make the buttercream, place the icing sugar in a large mixing bowl and beat in the butter and orange flower water until smooth. Ice the top of the cake with the buttercream and carefully place the crystallized petals on top.

Sherbet Sweetie Cake

This is every child's dream, and perhaps a dentist's nightmare, but it's only once a year. Your child will love you for this special treat, piled with lemon sherbet icing and sweeties.

200 g (7 oz) butter at room temperature

200 g (7 oz) caster sugar

3 large free-range eggs

1 teaspoon vanilla essence

300 g (10 oz) self-raising flour, sifted

Grated rind of 1 lemon

125 ml (4 fl oz) whole milk

Lemon sherbet icing

500 g (1 lb) icing sugar, sifted

100 g (3½ oz) butter at room temperature

150 g (5 oz) sherbet (available in tubes from sweet shops)

50 ml (2 fl oz) lemon juice

To decorate

Dolly beads

Lemon sherbets

Jelly beans

Jelly babies

Cola bottles

Serves 8–10

Baking time 30 minutes

1 Preheat the oven to 180°C (350°F), Gas Mark 4, and grease and line the bottoms of two 20 cm (8 inch) loose-bottomed cake tins. Lightly cream the butter until light and fluffy, then beat in the caster sugar until just combined. Beat in the eggs one at a time, followed by the vanilla essence. Gently fold in the flour, taking care not to overwork the mixture, then stir in the lemon rind and milk.

2 Divide the mixture between the tins and bake in the preheated oven for 30 minutes until a skewer inserted into the cakes comes out clean. Leave the cakes to cool before releasing them from the tins.

3 To make the icing, place the icing sugar in a large mixing bowl and beat in the butter and sherbet, then the lemon juice to make a smooth, creamy icing. Sandwich the cakes together with half the icing, then leave to set for 30 minutes.

4 Spread the remaining icing over the top of the cake, then pile with heaps of wonderful old-fashioned sweets.

Birthday Cupcakes

Both children and adults alike seem to love cupcakes, and they make a great display at any birthday party (see page 2). You could even personalize a cake for each individual guest using writing icing tubes.

1 Preheat the oven to 200°C (400°F), Gas Mark 6, and line two 12-hole muffin trays with paper cases. Lightly cream the butter until light and fluffy, then beat in the caster sugar until just combined. Beat in the eggs one at a time, followed by the vanilla essence. Gently fold in the flour, taking care not to overwork the mixture.

2 Divide the mixture between the paper cases and cook in the preheated oven for 20 minutes or until the cakes are golden. Leave to cool in the tins.

3 Divide the buttercream into a number of different bowls and colour each with a different food colouring, adding a little at a time until you reach the desired shade.

4 Once the cupcakes have cooled completely, ice the tops with buttercream and top with sprinkles and sugar flowers. Once the icing has dried slightly, pop the candles into the cakes.

250 g (8 oz) butter at room temperature

225 g (7½ oz) golden caster sugar

4 large free-range eggs

2 teaspoons vanilla essence

250 g (8 oz) self-raising flour, sifted

2 quantities Vanilla Buttercream (see page 113)

Pink, yellow, green and blue food colourings

To decorate

Sprinkles and sugar flowers

Birthday candles

Makes 24
Baking time 20 minutes

Princess birthday party

This is the perfect party for the little princess in all of us. Your little girl will enjoy this party with her friends, but you will also share great pleasure in creating the cutesy and girl heaven with her beforehand. I have devised ultimate girly edible treats, but all of them are simple to make and will not get you too stressed.

Pink is the colour of the day and a mixture of shades works well. Pink plates and cups are essential, arranged on a pink or lace tablecloth. Scatter the table with fairy dust (sequins or confetti to me or you), place pink roses tied with glittery ribbon in the centre of the table, and adorn each place setting with a fairy wand and princess tiara. Pink lemonade is essential, best served from a teapot and poured into real teacups to make the guests feel like proper little ladies!

A cost-effective and simple way to make party bags is to fill pink paper cups with sweets, nail varnishes, stamps or bath bubbles, then wrap each cup in pale pink netting and tie with a ribbon. Adorn with beaded heart decorations or trimmings for an extra special touch.

Princess party menu

♥

Fairy Bread (see page 120)

Strawberry Mousse Cake (see page 125)

Queen of Hearts Biscuits (see page 122)

White Chocolate-dipped Strawberries (see page 50)

Princess Cake (see page 126)

Pink Lemonade (see page 124)

Cowboy birthday party

Let your nostalgic side loose on this cowboy party, strictly for the boys! They will love these classic edible treats and will have a blast at playing cowboys all afternoon. Set the scene with the party table: choose a red and white chequered tablecloth, or you could source vintage cowboy prints. Red, green and brown are cowboy colours, so try to get plates, cups and napkins in these shades. Scatter the table with horse shoes and real mini cacti among the plates of cakes – try to get cacti without spikes to be safer. Chocolate coins and playing cards for cowboy poker games are also fun and add to the theme.

Each child should have a cowboy hat at their place setting, and you can serve ginger ale in glass bottles with straws, so the cowboys can enjoy some 'beer' fresh from the saloon!

Brown paper bags tied with red ribbon make great party bags. Alternatively, use squares of red and white chequered fabric tied with brown ribbon. Fill the bags with coloured sweets, rubber snakes, liquorice ropes, chocolate coins, plastic horses, mini harmonicas and sheriff's badges.

Cowboy party menu

♥

Star-shaped sandwiches (see page 10)

Party Popcorn Buckets (see page 32)

Apple Cactus Cupcakes (see page 130)

Chocolate Chip Cookies (see page 128)

Chocolate Nut No-bake Slices (see page 129)

Cowboy Ranch Cake (see page 132)

Carrot Cake (see page 88)

21st birthday party

The following ideas and menu will create a 21st party filled with glitz and glamour, but one that would suit either sex equally well. For your décor to ooze sophistication, stick to white or cream and silver as the theme, with lots of sparkle for the ultimate chic affair. Lay your tables with crisp white linen and adorn with silver stars and sequins, glitter, and crystal and pearl beads.

Place a large punch bowl in the centre of the table filled with our delicious Celebration Champagne Punch and use star-shaped place cards. For favours, decorate small silver boxes with silver star beads or sequins and fill with clear mint sweets, bubbles for blowing and crystal hanging decorations.

21st birthday menu

♥

Smoked Salmon Blinis (see page 136)

Cheese Stars (see page 137)

Champagne Cupcakes (see page 138)

Elderflower Tea Bread (see page 133)

Decadent White Chocolate Cake (see page 134)

Celebration Champagne Punch (see page 139)

Fairy Bread Hearts

No girly party would be the same without fairy bread, although boys seem to love it too and adults have been known to nibble... This party classic can be simply cut into triangles if you don't have heart-shaped cutters.

1 Spread the slices of bread with margarine on both sides, then use a biscuit cutter to cut out heart shapes.

2 Pour the hundreds and thousands onto a large plate, then dip the hearts in the sprinkles to cover evenly on both sides. Place the fairy bread hearts onto a clean plate ready to serve.

10 slices of soft white bread

Soft margarine, for spreading

1–2 pots of hundreds and thousands sprinkles

Makes 40

Queen of Hearts Biscuits

With their lovely Alice-in-Wonderland charm, these beautiful biscuits are perfect for a girly party, and fun to make with the children.

100 g (3½ oz) salted butter at room temperature

100 g (3½ oz) golden caster sugar

1 free-range egg

1 teaspoon almond essence

225 g (7½ oz) plain flour, sifted, plus extra for dusting

About 3 tablespoons strawberry jam

Icing sugar, for dusting

Makes 20
Baking time 18 minutes

1 Cream the butter until light and fluffy, then gently beat in the caster sugar until just combined. Beat in the egg and the almond essence, then mix in the flour until you have a soft dough. Form into a ball, wrap in clingfilm and chill for at least 1 hour.

2 Preheat the oven to 180°C (350°F), Gas Mark 4, and cover two baking sheets with baking parchment. Warm the dough a little in your hands. Lightly dust a work surface with flour and roll out the dough to approximately 4 mm (¼ inch) thick. Use a 6 cm (2½ inch) heart-shaped cutter to cut out 20 biscuits. Now use a smaller heart-shaped cutter to cut out the centres of the biscuits to form the windows. Carefully lift the heart frames onto one of the baking sheets using a spatula and cook in the preheated oven for 8 minutes until just golden at the edges.

3 Meanwhile, reroll all the trimmings and cut out 20 more large hearts to form the bottom layers of the biscuits. Transfer to the second baking sheet. After you have removed the first baking sheet from the oven, cook the second batch of biscuits for 10 minutes. Leave all the biscuits to cool on the sheets.

4 Spoon about ½ teaspoon of strawberry jam onto each solid heart, then place the heart frames on top. Leave the biscuits to set for 1 hour, then dust with icing sugar and serve.

Pink Lemonade

There's nothing like a refreshing glass of lemonade on a hot day. This is ideal for a child's birthday party, or even just to accompany afternoon tea.

250 g (8 oz) caster sugar
250 ml (8 fl oz) boiling water
Juice of 6 lemons
1 teaspoon grenadine syrup
1 litre (1¾ pints) cold water
Ice and lemon slices, to serve

Serves 6

1 Place the sugar and measured boiling water in a small saucepan over a medium heat and stir until all the sugar has dissolved. Remove from the heat and pour into a large jug.

2 Add the lemon juice and stir well, followed by the grenadine syrup. You can add a little more grenadine if you prefer a stronger colour.

3 Top up with the measured cold water and chill for at least 2 hours. Stir well before serving in glasses over ice, each decorated with a slice of lemon and a straw.

Strawberry Mousse Cake

This simple no-bake cake is rather like a cheesecake. It takes me back to when I was a teenager and my friend Kim and I made a different dessert every night for a month. Like this, they were all things that could be make with basic ingredients we had in the house.

1 Grease and line the bottom and sides of a 20 cm (8 inch) loose-bottomed cake tin. Mix the melted butter with the biscuit crumbs and press the mixture into the bottom of the tin to make an even layer.

2 Set a hand-held whisk on a medium speed and whisk the milk and mousse powder together until the mousse thickens. Whisk in the cream cheese until well combined and pour into the cake tin on top of the biscuit base. Level the surface and chill in the refrigerator for at least 6 hours until set.

3 Release the cake from the tin, top with sliced strawberries and drizzle with strawberry sauce.

100 g (3½ oz) butter, melted

200 g (7 oz) digestive biscuits, crushed into fine crumbs

600 ml (1 pint) milk

Strawberry mousse powder, enough for 600 ml (1 pint) milk

200 g (7 oz) cream cheese

8 strawberries, sliced

Strawberry ice-cream sauce, to drizzle

Serves 8–10

Princess Cake

This is a ridiculously girly cake, fit for a birthday princess. Her majesty will love the look and taste of this cake, which tastes even better when you're wearing a crown!

250 g (8 oz) butter at room temperature

250 g (8 oz) golden caster sugar

4 large free-range eggs

2 teaspoons strawberry flavouring

1 teaspoon pink food colouring

250 g (8 oz) self-raising flour, sifted

To fill and decorate

2 tablespoons strawberry jam

3 pink wafer biscuits, crushed

1 quantity Strawberry Buttercream (see page 84)

Icing sugar, for dusting

150 g (6 oz) bright pink ready-to-roll fondant icing

50 g (2 oz) pale pink ready-to-roll fondant icing

Edible gold balls

Edible pink and gold glitter

Serves 8–10
Baking time 25–30 minutes

1 Preheat the oven to 180°C (350°F), Gas Mark 4, and grease and line the bottoms of two 20 cm (8 inch) loose-bottomed cake tins. Cream the butter until light and fluffy, then beat in the caster sugar until just combined. Beat in the eggs one at a time, then add the strawberry flavouring and pink colouring. Gently fold in the flour, taking care not to overwork the mixture.

2 Divide the mixture between the prepared tins, level the surface and cook in the preheated oven for 25–30 minutes until a skewer inserted into the cakes comes out clean. Leave to cool in the tins.

3 Release the cakes and sandwich together with the jam and crushed wafer biscuits, then leave to set for 30 minutes. Use a palette knife to spread the buttercream over the cake.

4 Dust a work surface with icing sugar and roll out the bright pink fondant icing. Use a crown-shaped cutter or a cardboard template to cut out the crown shape and place it in the centre of the cake. Use a small heart-shaped cutter to cut out 24 hearts. Roll out the pale pink icing and cut out 5 large hearts. Arrange the hearts on the cake using the picture as a guide, use gold balls to make jewels on the crown, then scatter the cake with glitter.

Chocolate Chip Cookies

Everybody loves chocolate chip cookies. These have the perfect balance of crispy edge and chewy centre, in my opinion the essence of any cookie.

250 g (8 oz) butter at room temperature

150 g (5 oz) golden caster sugar

150 g (5 oz) light muscovado sugar

2 large free-range eggs

2 teaspoons vanilla essence

350 g (11½ oz) plain flour, sifted

1½ teaspoons baking powder

½ teaspoon salt

100 g (3½ oz) chocolate chips

Makes 18–20
Baking time 16 minutes

1 Preheat the oven to 180°C (350°F), Gas Mark 4, and cover 2 baking sheets with baking parchment.

2 Cream the butter until light and fluffy, then gently beat in the sugars until just combined. Beat in the eggs one at a time, followed by the vanilla essence, then mix in the flour, baking powder and salt until you have a soft dough. Fold in the chocolate chips, until they are evenly distributed in the dough.

3 Place heaped tablespoons of the dough on the baking sheets, spacing them well apart to leave room for them to spread. Cook in the preheated oven for 16 minutes, until golden. Leave to cool on the trays.

Chocolate Nut No-bake Slices

This is simplicity itself to prepare and requires no baking. The combination of peanut butter and chocolate is divine and deeply indulgent.

1 Grease and line the bottom and sides of a 20 cm (8 inch) square shallow tin. Place the crushed biscuits in a mixing bowl with the sugar and mix in the peanut butter to form a thick paste. Fold in the chocolate chips until evenly distributed.

2 Use your hands to press the mixture into an even layer in the bottom of the prepared tin and use the back of a spoon to smooth the surface.

3 Melt the chocolate and butter in a heatproof bowl over a saucepan of gently simmering water, stirring regularly. Pour the mixture over the peanut butter base and leave to cool at room temperature for 30 minutes. Place in the refrigerator for at least 2 hours to set.

4 Once fully hardened, cut into 16 slices while still in the tin. The mixture will be very hard, so dip your knife into boiling water before making each cut.

4 digestive biscuits, crushed into fine crumbs

100 g (3½ oz) light muscovado sugar

200 g (7 oz) smooth peanut butter

75 g (3 oz) chocolate chips

200 g (7 oz) milk chocolate, broken into pieces

50 g (2 oz) butter

Makes 16

Apple Cactus Cupcakes

These cupcakes have a lovely surprise apple centre, perfect for keeping little cowboys happy! The fondant cacti are a little fiddly, but a great addition to a cowboy party.

225 g (7½ oz) green ready-to-roll fondant icing

125 g (4 oz) butter at room temperature

100 g (3½ oz) golden caster sugar

2 large free-range eggs

1 teaspoon vanilla essence

125 g (4 oz) self-raising flour, sifted

200 g (7 oz) apple sauce (see below)

Drop of green food colouring

1 quantity Vanilla Buttercream (see page 113)

Makes 12
Baking time 20–25 minutes

1 Make the fondant cactus decorations the day before you make the cakes. Divide the green icing into 12 equal pieces and use your fingers to mould the cactus shapes. Lay the finished cacti on their sides on a baking sheet covered with baking parchment and leave to harden overnight.

2 The next day, preheat the oven to 200°C (400°F), Gas Mark 6 and line a 12-hole muffin tray with paper cases. Lightly cream the butter until light and fluffy, then beat in the sugar until just combined. Beat in the eggs one at a time, followed by the vanilla essence. Gently fold in the flour, taking care not to overwork the mixture.

3 Divide half of the mixture between the paper cases and top each with a teaspoon of apple sauce. Spoon the remaining cake mixture on top, taking care not to spread the apple sauce around as you want it to stay in the centres of the cakes. Cook in the preheated oven for 20–25 minutes until golden. Leave to cool in the tray.

4 Add a drop of green food colouring to the buttercream, then use the back of a teaspoon to spread it over the cakes and top each with a fondant cactus.

> ♥ **Tip:** *To make your own apple sauce, peel, core and chop 300 g (10 oz) Cox's apples and place in a saucepan with 2 tablespoons of water, 50 g (2 oz) of caster sugar and 1 teaspoon of lemon juice. Cover, bring to the boil and cook gently over a medium heat for about 15 minutes until the apples are tender. Leave to cool, then mash with a fork. Store any unused sauce in the refrigerator for up to 1 week.* ♥

Cowboy Ranch Cake

This chocolatey cake doubles up as something for the kids to take home – you can add a toy horse cake topper for each little cowboy to take with their slice of cake.

250 g (8 oz) butter at room temperature

225 g (7½ oz) golden caster sugar

4 large free-range eggs

2 teaspoons vanilla essence

250 g (8 oz) self-raising flour, sifted

2 heaped tablespoons cocoa powder

50 g (2 oz) crushed Maltesers

75 g (3 oz) Smarties

Malted chocolate icing

450 g (14½ oz) icing sugar, sifted

50 g (2 oz) cocoa, sifted

100 g (3½ oz) butter at room temperature

1 tablespoon malted milk drink powder

60 ml (2½ fl oz) water

To decorate

Smarties

Milk chocolate chips

8–10 plastic horse figures

4 green fondant cacti (see page 130)

Serves 8–10
Baking time 25 minutes

1 Preheat the oven to 180°C (350°F), Gas Mark 4, and grease and line the bottoms of two 20 cm (8 inch) loose-bottomed cake tins. Lightly cream the butter until light and fluffy, then beat in the caster sugar until just combined. Beat in the eggs one at a time, followed by the vanilla essence. Gently fold in the flour and cocoa, taking care not to overwork the mixture, then fold in the crushed Maltesers and Smarties until evenly distributed.

2 Divide the mixture between the tins and bake in the preheated oven for 25 minutes until a skewer inserted into the cakes comes out clean. Leave the cakes to cool before releasing them from the tins.

3 To make the buttercream, place the icing sugar and cocoa in a large mixing bowl and beat in the butter, malted milk powder and then the measured water to make a smooth, creamy icing. Sandwich the cakes together with half the buttercream, then leave to set for 30 minutes.

4 Use a palette knife to spread the remaining buttercream over the top of the cake. Decorate the cake with the scattering of Smarties and chocolate chips and position the plastic horses and fondant cacti to make a ranch scene.

Elderflower Tea Bread

This refreshing tea bread is lighter and fluffier than most, with the subtle but distinctive flavour of elderflower.

1 Preheat the oven to 180°C (350°F), Gas Mark 4, and grease and lightly flour a loaf tin, approximately 10 cm (4 inches) wide and 20 cm (8 inches) long.

2 Lightly cream the butter until light and fluffy, then beat in the sugar until just combined. Beat in the eggs one at a time, then gently fold in the flour. Fold in the elderflower cordial and sultanas until evenly distributed.

3 Spoon the mixture into the prepared tin, level the surface and cook in the preheated oven for 50 minutes until a skewer inserted into the cake comes out clean. Leave the cake to cool in the tin, then after about 30 minutes use a fork to make holes in the top of the cake. Drizzle a little elderflower cordial – about 2 tablespoons – over the top of the cake and leave to cool completely. Serve thickly sliced.

150 g (5 oz) butter at room temperature

125 g (4 oz) golden caster sugar

3 large free-range eggs

200 g (7 oz) self-raising flour, sifted

75 ml (3 fl oz) elderflower cordial, plus extra for drizzling

75 g (3 oz) sultanas

Serves 8–10
Baking time 50 minutes

Decadent White Chocolate Cake

This sumptuous cake is very rich, but fabulous. Perfect served with tea, or Champagne for a really special celebration.

200 g (7 oz) butter at room temperature

200 g (7 oz) golden caster sugar

3 large free-range eggs

1 teaspoon vanilla essence

125 ml (4 fl oz) whole milk

300 g (10 oz) self-raising flour, sifted

75 g (3 oz) white chocolate, roughly chopped

White chocolate buttercream

100 g (3½ oz) white chocolate, melted

50 g (2 oz) butter at room temperature

400 g (13 oz) icing sugar, sifted

4 teaspoons water

To decorate

25 g (1 oz) white chocolate

25 g (1 oz) white chocolate chips

Silver balls

Serves 8–10

Baking time 30 minutes

1 Preheat the oven to 180°C (350°F), Gas Mark 4, and grease and line the bottoms of two 20 cm (8 inch) loose-bottomed cake tins. Lightly cream the butter until light and fluffy, then beat in the caster sugar until just combined. Beat in the eggs one at a time, followed by the vanilla essence and milk. Gently fold in the flour and chopped white chocolate, taking care not to overwork the mixture.

2 Divide the mixture between the tins and cook in the preheated oven for 30 minutes until a skewer inserted into the cakes comes out clean. Leave the cakes in the tins to cool.

3 To make the buttercream, mix the melted chocolate with the butter in a large mixing bowl, then stir in the icing sugar and the water. Release the cakes from the tins and sandwich together using half the buttercream. Set aside for 30 minutes.

4 Use a potato peeler and the remaining chocolate to make chocolate shavings to decorate the cake. Spread the remaining buttercream over the top of the cake and top with the shavings, white chocolate chips and silver balls.

Smoked Salmon Blinis

The credit goes again to Leon for this, his blini recipe. These will really impress your guests, but little do they know how easy they are to make.

3 large free-range eggs, separated
125 ml (4 fl oz) double cream
75 g (3 oz) plain flour, sifted
Pinch of salt
About 2 tablespoons sunflower oil
100 ml (3½ fl oz) soured cream
50 g (2 oz) cream cheese
250 g (8 oz) smoked salmon
Handful of snipped chives

Makes 35–40

1　Cover a baking sheet with baking parchment. Whisk the egg yolks with the cream in a large mixing bowl, then stir in the flour to make a smooth paste. Use a hand-held electric whisk to whisk the egg whites with the salt in a separate bowl until they form soft peaks, then fold into the yolk mixture, one-third at a time. Fold very gently so you do not lose all the air you have whisked in.

2　Heat a large frying pan over a medium heat and add the sunflower oil, enough to lightly cover the base of the frying pan. When the oil is hot, spoon 1 tablespoon of the mixture into the pan to make a blini, and repeat to make 3 more if your pan is large enough. Cook the blinis for about 2 minutes, then turn and cook for a further 2 minutes until they are golden on both sides. Place the cooked blinis on the baking sheet to cool.

3　Reduce the heat slightly after your first batch and do not add any more oil. Continue cooking the blinis in batches of 4 until all the mixture has been used up.

4　Just before serving, mix the soured cream and cream cheese together and spoon a little onto the top of each cooled blini. Top with a sliver of smoked salmon and some snipped chives and serve immediately.

Cheese Stars

These are so versatile: the perfect fingerfood for parties, ideal for snacking and great for packed lunches. You can even pile them with toppings and serve as canapés.

1 Place the flour in a large mixing bowl, then rub in the butter with your fingertips until the mixture resembles fine breadcrumbs. Add the grated cheese and stir to combine.

2 Make a well in the centre and pour in the beaten egg and measured water. Mix with a wooden spoon, starting from the centre of the well and stirring outwards until you have a sticky dough. Gather the dough into a disc, wrap in cling film and chill in the refrigerator for 1 hour.

3 Preheat the oven to 180°C (350°F), Gas Mark 4, and cover two baking sheets with baking parchment. Lightly dust a work surface with flour, then roll out the dough to approximately 1 cm (½ inch) thick and cut out stars with a 4 cm (1¾ inch) star-shaped cutter, rerolling the trimmings as necessary. Place on the prepared baking sheets and brush with beaten egg. Bake in the preheated oven for 10 minutes until golden. Leave to cool on the trays for at least 30 minutes before serving.

100 g (3½ oz) chilled butter, cubed

100 g (3½ oz) plain flour, sifted, plus extra for dusting

125 g (4 oz) mature Cheddar cheese, grated

1 free-range egg, beaten, plus extra for glazing

2–3 tablespoons water

Makes 40
Baking time 10 minutes

♥ **Tip:** *Cheese Stars are great for serving as canapés. Either serve them plain or use them as a base and top with a small spoon of crème fraîche and a few snipped chives, or a dollop of cream cheese and a slice of cherry tomato.* ♥

Champagne Cupcakes

Perfect for a glamorous event, this is the ultimate celebration cupcake – best served with Champagne of course.

125 g (4 oz) butter at room temperature

125 g (4 oz) golden caster sugar

2 large free-range eggs

150 g (5 oz) self-raising flour, sifted

50 ml (2 fl oz) Champagne

12 cream-coloured sugar rosebuds, to decorate

Champagne buttercream

500 g (1 lb) icing sugar, sifted

100 g (3½ oz) butter at room temperature

50 ml (2 fl oz) Champagne

Makes 12
Baking time 20 minutes

1   Preheat the oven to 200°C (400°F), Gas Mark 6, and line a 12-hole muffin tray with paper cases. Lightly cream the butter until light and fluffy, then beat in the caster sugar until just combined. Beat in the eggs one at a time. Gently fold in the flour, taking care not to overwork the mixture, then fold in the Champagne until well mixed.

2   Divide the mixture between the paper cases and cook in the preheated oven for 20 minutes until golden. Leave to cool in the tray.

3   To make the buttercream, place the icing sugar in a large mixing bowl, then beat in the butter and then the Champagne to make a smooth, creamy icing. Use the back of a teaspoon to spread the icing over the cakes and top each with a sugar rosebud.

Celebration Champagne Punch

The gorgeous slices of star fruit floating in this punch make it so pretty, ideal for a celebration party table.

1 Choose a large serving bowl for your punch, but make sure it will fit into your refrigerator. Pour the Triple Sec and white rum into the bowl and top with the pineapple juice. Stir in the ginger ale, then chill in the refrigerator for several hours.

2 Just before serving, slice the star fruits across the width to show their beautiful star shapes. Pour the chilled Champagne into the punch bowl and add some ice. Float the star fruits and grapes on top of the punch and serve in small glasses.

250 ml (8 fl oz) Triple Sec

250 ml (8 fl oz) white rum

500 ml (17 fl oz) pineapple juice

1 litre (1¾ pints) ginger ale

6 star fruits

2 bottles of Champagne, chilled

Bunch of white seedless grapes, halved

Ice cubes, to serve

Serves 15–20

Index

Acknowledgements

I would like to thank Jonas, my right hand man and a true friend, who can make my cakes better than me – without him I wouldn't be here. To Yolandi, who we continue to miss every day. To Leon for always making me laugh. To Michelle, Ana, Natalie and Cecilia – bake-a-boo girls forever. To my mum and dad for allowing me to live my dream, and my very special sister for always being there for me. To Luke for true help and advice. To my Kylan and Cosmo for being great tasters! To dearest Celia and Pippa for their time and kindness. To everyone at Bacchus for making me believe my cupcakes were special in the first place. To Samantha Flower for changing my life and perhaps making me start this business. To my friends for supporting me through the hard times, especially Amar for being a true star. To Joan Scarrott for inspiring me. To Alexandra Palace farmers market – where bake-a-boo was born! To all my fellow Mill Lane traders and finally to the lovely people of West Hampstead who have supported us and kept my dream alive.